ALOYSIUS

"St. Aloysius Gonzaga," original silhouette by Dan Paulos, Albuquerque, New Mexico

ALOYSIUS

Edited by
Clifford Stevens and William Hart McNichols

Our Sunday Visitor Publishing Division
Our Sunday Visitor, Inc.
Huntington, Indiana 46750

Our Sunday Visitor Publishing Division
Our Sunday Visitor, Inc.
200 Noll Plaza
Huntington, Indiana 46750

International Standard Book Number: 0-87973-528-7
Library of Congress Catalog Card Number: 92-61552

Jacket illustration: Icon, "St. Aloysius Similar to Fire" by William Hart
McNichols, S.J. Cover imprint: facsimile signature of St. Aloysius Gonzaga

PUBLISHED AND PRINTED IN THE UNITED STATES OF AMERICA

528

DEDICATION

To Father Clifford Stevens, priest and devoted contemplative, friend of Saint Aloysius, and initiator of this gift of love in the official "Aloysian Year of 1991-92."

ACKNOWLEDGMENTS

The editors wish to thank the editor of *The Homiletic and Pastoral Review* for permission to reprint "Four Centuries of Aloysius" by Clifford Stevens, and the editor of *The Jesuit Bulletin* for permission to reprint "St. Aloysius: Patron of Youth" by William Hart McNichols, S.J., as adapted in this work.

CONTENTS

"St. Aloysius with Plague Victim," sculpture by Pierre Legros fils (1666-1719), in Rome

Fourth Centenary of the Death of Saint Aloysius Gonzaga

In the concluding months of the Ignatian Year, the calendar of historic events turns the spotlight to the death, four centuries ago — on 21 June, 1591 — of Aloysius Gonzaga, eldest son of the Marquis of Castiglione and scholastic of the Society of Jesus. The diocese of Mantua, Italy, has declared this an "Aloysian Year," and the Holy Father himself will take part in the celebrations the day of the liturgical feast in the Saint's native town and diocese.

The moment the name of Aloysius Gonzaga is pronounced, people seem to place themselves on the defensive. His witness of holiness is easily branded as not meant for imitation. If we are to believe some people, it would be almost a counter-testimony of Ignatian spirituality, open as this is to the world and its challenges, ever on the front line in the encounter of the Gospel with modern times. In spite of the effort made by authors of repute to present, especially to the young, the true likeness of this Saint, does he not continue to be inevitably consigned to those who belong to another age, indeed to another world? In the attempt to present him in an acceptable manner, we run the risk of depriving Aloysius Gonzaga of what constitutes his greatness, that of being a true son of Ignatius while being the noble son of a distinguished family, related to so many princes, cardinals, and popes, a rebel against his own milieu, a brave and loyal subject of the true King, following him in his young Society. Aloysius draws all the consequences of this companionship, not only by going against established custom, but also by radically adopting the life of the poor in the footsteps of Christ the poor, always surrounded by the poor.

At the beginning, he begs in order to distribute among the poor the money he collects in alms. But he goes further and achieves a veritable insertion by being close to the poor and the unfortunate in the hospitals, no matter his repugnance at the sight of blood and wounds. At the end he will devote his life to the poor, helping out the worst among the plague-stricken, those abandoned in the streets of Rome. Thus he was not content to follow the Lord of the poor with words or generous intentions; in the best tradition of the *Spiritual Exercises*, he expressed his joy for having been placed with the Son in the concrete trials of everyday life, in the painful reality of his time, the plague. Through these gestures of Aloysius Gonzaga, the Lord of life continued to be present among the unfortunate, a living blessing and beatitude. No wonder, then, that the AIDS victims of several countries have quite spontaneously recognized in him their intercessor, and the picture of Aloysius Gonzaga carrying on his shoulders the victims of this modern plague is spreading. The Roman hospital in which Aloysius Gonzaga performed his ministry keeps to this day the memory of these glad tidings of salvation, this witness to Christ the Savior. The undeniable force of his life in the Spirit, far from taking him away from reality, drives him to love unto the end those who are in the world, just as Christ did. And so we do not have to offer apologies for the incomparable life of Aloysius Gonzaga, but rather for not recognizing in him a genuine representative of Ignatian spirituality, very naturally and very supernaturally. If we go to the essentials of his witness, we shall not fail to discover a fellow brother, a stirring example, a praying intercessor in Aloysius Gonzaga.

May Aloysius Gonzaga be celebrated like a true son of Ignatius during this Ignatian Year. His evangelical radicality was emphasized by our revered Father Pedro Arrupe with these words at the time of the fourth centenary of the birth of Aloysius Gonzaga: "Aloysius does not bargain, he does not compromise; he cannot share in the distortions of Christ made by the world and by society. If the world denies Christ, he accepts him and follows him totally."

Peter-Hans Kolvenbach
Superior General, the Society of Jesus

Rome, 22 May, 1991

Aluigi Gonzaga:
The Lotus Sutra

Aloysius,
is there a single
secret or seed
of the kingdom
you do not know
or bear
within?
Born in a most
arrogant time,
when belief in the self
and all that one
could do
had tilted minds
and faces like
elegant Botticellis
to the new gods
who peered from
the convex and
concave mirrors of the
High Renaissance.
In the painted, sculpted
images of you,
however,
one can still see
the precocious boy
who taught simply,
like the Lost Child,
from the starched
ruff and collar

of your brief
childhood.
Or in Guercino's
masterpiece, you are
a lambent flame,
flickering and burning
neath a smoke of
singing angels
before the
Capuchin cross.
Or in hospitals and hospices
you are captured as
Legros's healing boy,
carrying the sick and dying;
youthful midwife to the
second birth,
watching souls pass
like spirit birds
into the Light
of His presence.
And then you are
happily home,
perched on the clouds,
waving a shaft of lilies,
and smiling,
from Pozzo's
trompe l'oeil skies.
But in the shadows
of my night,
when I cannot find
your smile or
the harbor of your wings,
when I fear my limbs
and will
are clay,
I remember you
also grew

from silt and sludge,
and then suddenly . . .
you appear as the
flowering lotus,
and this sutra
is all I need
touch and know and hear
of you for
now.

William Hart McNichols, S.J.

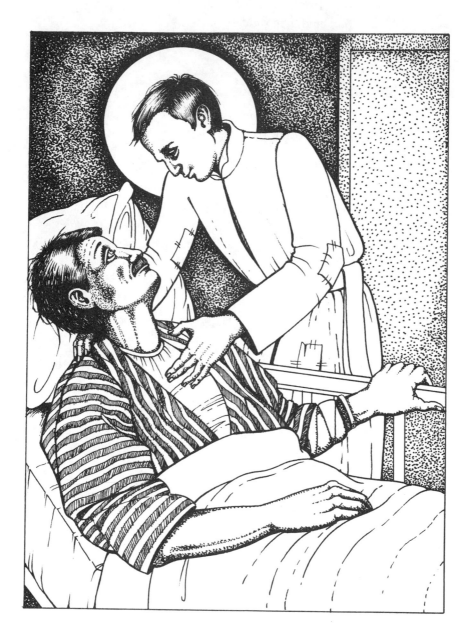

"St. Aloysius Gonzaga, Friend of the Sick," drawing by William Hart McNichols

I

Four Centuries of Aloysius

Clifford Stevens

It was in November of 1585 that Aloysius Gonzaga entered the Jesuit novitiate in Rome, after a fierce struggle, with a determination that set the whole of Italy ablaze with gossip and with admiration. On his arrival in Rome, with that courtesy that was part of his breeding, he visited relatives who were cardinals and others who were friends of his family, and had a short audience with Pope Sixtus V, who reminded him of the difficulties of religious life. Aloysius listened to everyone, made short comments about his decision, and finally was left alone in his room in the Jesuit novitiate on the Quirinal.

"This is my rest forever and ever," he said as he entered; "here will I dwell, for I have chosen it."

These were no empty words, nor were they merely an appropriate phrase taken from Scripture. They were literally true, for no one had *chosen* his vocation as had Aloysius Gonzaga, that vocation that was the end of his heart's desire and the fulfillment of all his dreams. But it had been a struggle and a battle, bowed down as he was with reverence for God and the love of Christ, and with an intense horror for the Renaissance court life that he had left behind.

1

There is in Aloysius Gonzaga a toughness hidden behind his gentle courtesy and complete self-effacement, a toughness that grew out of his struggle with his environment. His choice of the religious life, and the Jesuits in particular, was symbolic of his complete rejection of the way of life into which he had been born, and his arrival in Rome was, for him, the final act of deliverance from something that had become a millstone around his neck. He had prayed for that deliverance, struggled for it, fought for it with all the energy of his soul, and just a few months before it had seemed that deliverance would never come, as his father refused, then gave, then refused permission for him to renounce his princedom.

On his way to Rome, after he signed the papers that relieved him of his succession to the Gonzaga power, title, and fortune, someone remarked to him that his brother Rodolfo, who was now the heir and successor, must be delighted at the stroke of good fortune giving him all this. "Not half so glad as I am to be rid of it!" was Aloysius' reply. To the nobility of Renaissance Italy, he was a "monstrosity," casting aside with careless abandon what every one of them dreamed of possessing. His motivation was completely beyond them, but his motivation had been fashioned, tested, and tried in a struggle for freedom that is one of the great dramas of holiness.

It is hard for us in the twentieth century to realize the moral depravity and corruption of a Renaissance court, but some indication of the solidity of Aloysius' judgment is found in the history of his own princedom after his death. His brother Rodolfo murdered and was himself murdered; another brother died in his mother's arms after a cruel attack on both of them; and the history of the family is one of gross immorality, violence, vendetta, and raw ambition. Within a few short years, the princedom itself was lost forever in the dynastic battles that followed Aloysius' own death in 1591, and the name of Gonzaga today is a mere memory in Italian history, except for its association with him whom the Italians call "*San Luigi*."

Aloysius' realization of the path he would most likely follow as a Renaissance prince came to him when he was scarcely seven years old. During his First Confession, he saw where certain seemingly innocent acts of childhood mischief might have led him. He saw himself on a path of "no-restraint," his every whim and wish satisfied, and from that moment he began to fight against his own inherited lifestyle and drew upon deep inner resources remarkable for one so young. He was scarcely in Rome, with all of that behind him, when his brother Rodolfo began to follow just such a path of "no-restraint," and against his deepest desires, Aloysius found himself again embroiled in the affairs of his family.

The caliber of the man is seen in a brutally frank letter that he wrote to his brother after he had brought peace to the family, demanding some kind of honorable action on the part of his brother. (Rodolfo was living with a woman not his wife, and Aloysius demanded that he right the matter). Written in the inflated style of the period, the content of the letter is forceful and pointed, showing something of Aloysius' remarkable character:

"I intend to act as follows," wrote Aloysius. "I will wait for twelve days, beginning from tomorrow, for your answer. When I receive it, and if it is as it should be . . . I shall return happy to Rome. But if you act otherwise . . . I shall wind up the matter in the way I have indicated. . . . So do not fail to do your duty; do not fail; do not fail. Notice that I have said it three times. For without a doubt, if you fail, you will certainly regret it."

While he was still alive, Aloysius could restrain his younger brother, but after his death, Rodolfo carried out blood vendettas, was himself murdered, and was buried in unconsecrated ground. Aloysius' judgment on the pathway he himself might have followed was startlingly accurate.

2

Very early, Aloysius began to search for ways that could free him from the trap into which he had been born. He thought of everything: he would renounce his titles and become a hermit in one of his castles; he looked at the various religious orders of his time and found that most of them were stepping stones to honors and dignities he wanted to be free of. Some of his relatives were cardinals and archbishops, one of them Saint Charles Borromeo, who gave him his First Communion. Another relative, Hannibal Gonzaga, was a Franciscan, but he saw this cousin elected the head of his order, and another cousin, Scipio Gonzaga, made cardinal. Wherever he looked, he saw no escape from the kind of life he had come to despise. And then his father was called to Spain to the court of Philip II, and Aloysius became a page to the heir of the throne, Don Diego.

This involved him more and more in court life, and at one point, he was selected to give an address to King Philip himself, a minor piece of oratory that is humorous to read since it contains so little of

Aloysius' own feelings. It is in the stylized oratory of the day, with literary and historical references that were customary.

However, with the death of Don Diego, Aloysius considered his court duties done, and on a walk with his brother and their attendants, he stopped at the Jesuit College in Madrid and refused to budge. He had already revealed to his father that he wanted to be a Jesuit, and his father had fallen into one of his violent rages, threatening to have Aloysius flogged. Already he recognized the caliber of his oldest son and was determined to have him succeed him. He most probably recognized as well the lack of character in the younger son.

The older Gonzaga was sick with the gout and burdened down with gambling debts when Aloysius gave this display of spirit, and it took several trips by court officials to bring him home — the final inducement being that if he were going to leave, he should leave from his own house and not disgrace the family by this kind of public rebellion. With that, Aloysius went home.

Promising that when the family returned to Italy Aloysius might do as he pleased, the Marquis of Gonzaga took his family home. It was spring of 1584. Aloysius was sixteen years old.

The next year and a half was a battle of wills between Aloysius and his father. The two brothers were sent on a grand tour of their relatives, dressed in their finest clothes, with servants and carriages and all the pomp of the princely class. Aloysius discarded the fine clothes, dressed himself in black and kept to himself during most of the trip. He managed to visit a number of Jesuit houses on the way and firmly refused to attend banquets, dances, and plays. By his actions, this sixteen-year-old, in Father Martindale's words, was "flinging his glove" in the face of the court life that he so despised. He had pledged himself to a different kind of kingdom, and he wanted to make it very clear where his allegiance lay.

He returned after several months to the family headquarters at Castiglione, and here his father called in everyone capable of persuading Aloysius to change his mind: bishops, priests, uncles, cousins, dukes, cardinals, and members of religious orders. Aloysius held firm. In anger, his father ordered him from the house.

Apparently the whole of Italy, and even the church officials in Rome, had heard of the battle between father and son, and they waited and watched. Finally, after his father told Aloysius that he was too sickly to enter religious life and that he would not consider giving permission until Aloysius was at least twenty-five years old, Aloysius took the offensive in another way.

Bursting into his father's room, his father sick in bed, he told him: "Father, I place myself entirely in your hands. Do as you want with me. But know for certain that I have been called by God to the Society of Jesus, and in resisting this vocation you are resisting God." Faced with this startling assertion, his father gave in. Preparations were made for Aloysius to abdicate his princedom, his titles, and all claim to the succession. Aloysius had won.

3

Burning at the core of Aloysius' mind and heart was a hunger for God that literally tore his whole being apart. It was a hunger that had been born of a self-discipline fashioned for the sake of sheer survival, as he began to sense the depravity and moral corruption with which he was surrounded. In his anguish he had turned desperately to prayer, realizing that he could be swept into the torrent if he depended on his own powers. First he learned to pray with his lips and on his knees, and then a remarkable book came into his hands teaching him that he could *think* about God and occupy his mind with Him. He began to practice this kind of *thinking*, delighted in it and determined that, though sin was all around him, it would have no part of him. But with this *thinking* about God came something else. A desire to be *holy*. To be pleasing to God in every inch of his being. To be holy in body and soul, to belong totally to God.

This was the first glimmering of his vocation, and it never left him. He found it in Florence, where his father had sent him when he was ten years old, to be introduced to the courtesies and refinements of court life. With his little book in hand, he went to the altar of the Annunziata in the Servite Church there, and before the altar of Mary in that church he pondered on the vision of holiness that had taken hold of his mind, with a hunger for God that was the root of it, and there determined that this would be his life's goal. And he saw with startling clarity that his first task was to protect himself from the evil he saw around him. He was afterwards to say that it was in this chapel that his spiritual life had been born. From this moment on, there was no turning back.

He was sent to the court of the Duke of Mantua with his brother Rodolfo, living in the palace of a relative with a private chapel. He discovered the Psalms and the lives of the saints. He became sick, had to diet, and from this learned to fast, finding this a way to celebrate feast days, or at least to prepare for them. He had stumbled on the ascetic life and found in it a strange kind of freedom.

But at the same time he began to despair that he would ever be able to leave the court life that was his destiny as a prince of the Gonzagas. He looked around for ways to flee it, and he found himself deeper in prayer. It was at this time that he first thought about abdicating his succession, but he saw no way to do it, and he fled in the only direction he could go: into the arms of God. When he returned to his father's castle in Castiglione when he was twelve, he gave himself to prayer with an intensity noticed by all around him.

He trained himself to *think*, to concentrate on God, and for this he must have drawn upon the military training that he saw going on all around him. He had been born in his father's castle at Castiglione, had been the favorite of his father's soldiers, and as a very small boy had been outfitted with a miniature soldier's armor and weapons. He had even taken on something of the barracks' language when he was only five years old, only to be sternly told by his tutor that gentlemen did not use that kind of language. Training was part of his blood, and so he trained himself to think about God, first for an hour at a time, and soon he did not have to count the minutes.

He was simply overwhelmed with the reality of God, and then, quite by accident, a book by Peter Canisius came into his hands, one of his famous "summas" of Christian Doctrine, with an orderly set of meditations. This became a sort of meditation "training manual" for him, opening up vistas to his mind and making him something of a theologian. What happened next was something of a marvel for him and came about because of a visit of his illustrious cousin Charles Borromeo, Archbishop of Milan, one of the most remarkable churchmen of the day.

After a long conversation with Aloysius, the Cardinal discovered that he had not made his First Communion. He himself instructed the boy, and with this reception of the Eucharist, Aloysius found a center for his life that deepened his hunger for God. For the rest of his life, he could not come into that Presence without being rapt in prayer, and sometimes, in his later Jesuit days, he would break into a run as he approached the chapel. But at the age of twelve, he had no idea where his hunger for God would lead, and he began to ask God in those desperate tones that revealed something of his agony: "Direct me!"

When Aloysius first mentioned to his father his intention of becoming a Jesuit, his father thought it was a trick to make him stop gambling. The elder Gonzaga had lost a fortune gambling, and his relatives became concerned about the family's fortune. They hinted that Aloysius was afraid that none of his father's fortune would be left for his own inheritance and so was holding over his father's head the threat of becoming a Jesuit to make his father change his habits.

The father, Ferrante, half-believed it, since he had directed Aloysius a number of times to write to his relatives to keep his creditors off his back. One of these letters reveals the keen intelligence and practical sense of Aloysius, at about the age of fourteen, when he wrote for his father when they were in Spain:

> "My father is seriously ill with the gout in his hands, and so he is prevented from writing. By his order and direction, I am writing to recommend to you the affair you are familiar with [the demands of the creditors] . . . who continually molest my father and want at all costs to be paid, threatening him with the confiscation of his goods, to the ruin and scandal of our family. The heavy expenses here at Court make it impossible for him to take care of the obligation now as his creditors demand. I beg you to do something about it."

But once the idea had taken hold and Aloysius had decided on the Society of Jesus — nothing would turn him back. It fitted his idea of his vocation perfectly: there would be no honors and dignities, not even ecclesiastical, since the Constitutions forbade it; it was a life of poverty, modeled on that of Christ Himself, and it had a missionary and educational purpose. Besides, it was a new order with a first fervor that had not grown cold. By the very imagery of the Society, he would be enlisted in the Army of Christ and under His kingship. That was the only *Kingdom* he wished to belong to. When his father found that he could not dissuade him from this, Aloysius was free.

<h1 style="text-align:center">4</h1>

Today, four centuries after he entered on his vocation, it is his hunger for God and his strength of character that ring through every event of his short life. He entered the Jesuits at the age of seventeen and died scarcely twenty-three years old, the treasure he had grasped at the age of seven, his God, firmly in his grasp, held to with a tenacity that impressed the wise and learned Robert Bellarmine, his spiritual director and confessor, himself a giant of holiness and a shrewd judge of character:

> "God . . . taught us through the miracle of his life that there is no such thing as coming of age with Him, for boys and girls can beat us graybeards in the race to perfection. Let us thank God, Who lit for our guidance such an eager and splendid flame, and let us keep our eyes on it while our dark journey lasts."

But that life was lived against the history and politics of the age, of which Aloysius was a leading actor, swept up in the cruelty and lust and violence of Renaissance Italy, where conscience was little known and murder a way of life and every form of vice was cultivated, applauded, and given respectability. Aloysius *knew* what was expected of him; he saw it in the palaces and courts that he had to frequent, and he saw it dramatized as well in the theatricals originated by his family which became the rage of the courts of France and Spain and England.

With his whole being, he rejected this kind of life, and in his desperation, he flung himself into the arms of God and never turned his gaze back again. It is this kind of determination and this kind of tenacity that ring out of his life and that make him a part of our own turbulent century. He has something to say to the young, and he has something to say to the "graybeards," even now, four centuries after he won his battle and enrolled under the standard of Christ.

II

Aloysius Gonzaga: Role Model for Today's Young?

Walter J. Burghardt, S.J.

Toward the close of a twelve-year stint as theologian-in-residence at Georgetown University, I developed a particular interest in one aspect of Aloysius. In 1729 Pope Benedict XIII proclaimed him special patron of all students throughout the world; in 1926 Pope Pius XI declared him patron of all Christian youth, entreated young men to hold him always as their model. My question: Does that distinctive designation make sense today? Is there any solid reason why, say, a Georgetown lad or lass should find in Aloysius a pattern for contemporary living, specifically for college or university life — yes, even pray to him apart from exam-time desperation? To answer with some measure of persuasiveness, let me (1) set the problem in proper context, (2) speak at some length about Aloysius, and (3) link that young man to our young men and women today.

I

First, the problem in context. The context is contemporary spirituality. What is the significance of yesterday's saint for today's Christian?

On broad lines, three solutions may be suggested: two extremes and a middle. One extreme insists that usually the lives of the saints are normative for us: what they did, we must do. This imitation the Church herself would seem to recommend in her official prayers — in the liturgy of the Mass and in the prayer book we call the breviary. We are to "imitate what we revere" in the protomartyr Stephen, his spirit of forgiveness; we are to "follow continually the faith" of the

23

apostle Thomas, "imitate the actions" of Paul the first hermit, "follow" adolescent Agnes of Rome "by our virtuous way of life," "follow avidly the advice and example" of Peter Damiani. What we revere in the saints, this we ought to imitate.

The other extreme affirms that the saints of yesterday have little or nothing to say to contemporary man and woman. Those men and women lived, for the most part, in ages unlike our own. The situations in which they achieved sanctity are never quite repeated today. Their experiences and inner dynamisms are not reflected in our own. Read the lives of the saints, from John the Baptist and Ignatius of Antioch, through Perpetua and Felicity, Patrick and Boniface, to Martin de Porres and Thérèse of Lisieux, and you find yourself in other worlds — fascinating history, often impressively heroic, but too different from the modern age to be genuinely relevant. Revere the saints, yes; imitate them, no.

The position that underlies this article is in the nature of a *via media*, a centrist approach, an effort to harmonize and unify the valid insights of both extremes. In this approach the saints do have something precious to say to us, but their appeal is not to slavish imitation. In other words, the details that dot their lives may well be outmoded, dictated by ephemeral circumstances. Antony of Egypt locking himself in an Egyptian tomb; Martin de Porres asking his superior to sell him into slavery; Patrick praying on a snowcapped mountain; Aquinas casting his theology in song; Canisius hammering away relentlessly at heresy; Xavier dying alone six miles from China; Agnes leaving life for her faith at twelve or thirteen; all those saints who never bathed, refused to lift their eyes, slept rarely, ate reluctantly — it is not this that calls for imitation. Even when the finger of God is clearly there, these are individual actions, personal manifestations of inner drives, historically conditioned expressions of faith and love.

In this connection I am reminded of theologian Karl Rahner's insistence that "following" the Crucified is not simply synonymous with "imitating" him. "Imitate" has indeed precious precedent in Paul: "Be imitators of me, as I am of Christ" (1 Cor. 11:1). Still, as Rahner saw so clearly,

. . . we are not really expected to copy and reproduce the life of Jesus as such. We live in historical situations different from those in which Jesus himself lived, we have a different and always unique task which is not the same as that which confronted him in his own historically conditioned and restricted existence; he and we together form the one Christ of the one and unique total history of salvation, in which, for all our crucial dependence on him and on his historical existence in life and death, we do not reproduce him, but (as Paul says) complete his historical individual reality. . . .[1]

The point is that in the lives of all graced human persons there are realizations of faith, hope, and love which in his restricted life Jesus did not and could not experience. He was a man, not a woman; he was a teacher, but not a scholar; he did not experience old age or Alzheimer's disease; he never even lived to be a Jesuit!

If Jesus himself does not call for slavish imitation, literal reproduction, even less do the saints who "followed" him. This is not to disparage the details of their lives. For even in their highly personalized actions the saints do speak to us. The lives of the saints, or aspects of their lives, or individual episodes in their lives, even legends surrounding saints who did or did not exist — these illustrate in striking fashion certain principles or facets of Christian spirituality that are permanently valid, that have a relevance transcending persons and places, eras and situations. Even where saintly actions seem embarrassingly eccentric or bizarre, they often lend credence to Gilbert K. Chesterton's contention, "A saint is one who exaggerates what the world and the Church have forgotten."[2]

Basically, therefore, what the saints set before us for reproduction is not this or that detail of their lives, often historically conditioned, occasionally bizarre, but living examples of Christian *principles*, Christlike *approaches* to real-life situations, Gospel *motivations* that are abiding, that do not lose their validity with the passage of time, that shine through the variable concrete manifestations.

II

My second task is to illustrate my conviction from the life of Aloysius Gonzaga. In harmony with my thesis, I am not concerned to show that the details of his short life of twenty-three years form a mosaic that contemporary youth should reproduce. I intend to indicate how his life, for all its distance from us in centuries and character, can speak mutely and eloquently to teenagers and young adults today.

The Jesuit Desmond Reid expressed our problem insightfully thirty-six years ago. He noted that, broadly speaking, "we carry about with us a mental picture of the saints as they appeared towards the close of their years on earth": Francis Xavier the missionary to the East, silver-haired Pope Pius X, Francis de Sales the kindly bishop and director of souls.[3]

Aloysius has suffered much from this tendency of ours. It might be said that, as far as natural appeal goes, he died at an awkward age. At twenty-three he is an "in-between." He lacks the sparkle and charm of Stanislaus Kostka and Dominic Savio, and in comparison with these fresh and smiling stars he is, to many, a rather frosted moon. On the other hand there is wanting the mature touch of Xavier or Pius or Francis and other elder brothers in holiness. Yet to picture him as a black-robed, rather bleak-faced young religious, towering against a vacant sky, is to see less than half the man. It is to suggest an isolated, unfriendly figure, devoid of the human attractiveness which helps us to love the saints. In fairness to him, you must look to the circumstances; you must roll back the years; you must paint in the background, taking account of the riotous times in which he lived; and, above all, you must remember that he was a Gonzaga, for that was in many respects the key to his life. . . .[4]

A rather frosted moon. Yes, if you focus on individual facets, episodes, incidents, Aloysius can easily turn the adolescent off, the teenager, the young adult. I know that once, when playing forfeits, he refused to kiss the shadow of a girl in the game; that he was at one time called a "woman-hater." I read that at twelve or thirteen he slept on boards, wore spurs about his waist, flogged himself with strips of leather. I note that, though a prince, he avoided functions and festivities at the Spanish court of Philip, kept his eyes modestly down when he had to be present. I see that he simply refused to attend the theater, "what the French Parliament considered to be a high-school of adultery."[5] I sense that he carried fasting to an extreme, even after medicinal dieting played havoc with his digestive system. I recall that he almost burned himself to death in bed because he fell asleep in prayer. I find that in his six Jesuit years he obeyed every slightest wish of superiors with perhaps exaggerated meticulousness.

In these and other episodes and habits I find little to tempt the religious appetite of a teenager or collegian. On the other hand, two facets of his life and personality must be highlighted if we are to understand Aloysius and perhaps suggest his contemporaneity. One feature marks his pre-Jesuit life, the other closes his earthbound existence.

From early adolescence, Aloysius was a Gonzaga who "wanted out." Recall his position, his potential power. For almost four centuries (1328-1707) Gonzaga was the ruling family of Mantua. On the credit side, the Gonzagas produced able governors, built churches as well as palaces, commissioned magnificent art, and made Mantua a center of culture. Less admirably, you discover an adulterous wife beheaded, rapacious rulers, unbridled power, internecine hatred, human menageries; artistic sense wedded to bloodthirstiness, immorality to faith; a Niccolò d'Este, with eight hundred mistresses, beheading son and second wife on a single night; tyrants born out of wedlock, adored and murdered by their subjects; and so on, through seemingly endless corruption.

From age five on, Aloysius was hustled from camp to court, from one court to another — that "education of a prince" which often meant spiritual devastation. Apparently he was quite gifted intellectually: highly competent in the classics, even more interested in mathematics and astronomy, knowledgeable about the Spanish Empire, enamored of that facet of philosophy which dealt with God, arguing in debate that the Trinity could be known from naked human reason. He had an innate talent for diplomacy. In his teens he went on "business" trips for his gouty father.

An imperial prince, Aloysius was his father's pride and joy — a father who saw in this son the fulfillment of all his secular hopes, the only son fit to succeed him, to govern his estates and cities, to be a singular statesman, to lend a fresh glamour to the Gonzaga name. With this future in his plans, the idea of Jesuit life — poverty, chastity, obedience — for his favorite son plunged him into a rage. He threatened to flog him, announced that if Aloysius became a Jesuit he would no longer be his son. Then a fresh, more seductive strategy: Why not become a secular priest? Look at the good a Borromeo does. The Duke of Mantua promised him any ecclesiastical dignity in his power. When all this failed, his father ordered Aloysius out of his house, out of his sight. Finally, after all sorts of fluctuations, after years of tears and threats, we find a remarkable letter from this Marquis of Castiglione delivered by Aloysius to Claudius Acquaviva, superior general of the Society of Jesus, dated November 3, 1585:

> . . . In the past I considered it to be my duty to refuse to this my son Aloysius permission to enter your holy Society, for I feared that owing to his youth he might embark upon his enterprise without that firm resolution which were right. Now I think that I am sure that it is God who is calling him thither, and so I should feel it on my conscience were I to refuse him the permission that he has longed to receive, and has prayed for from me so urgently and so often. So, freely and willingly, with my mind at peace and full of God's good consolation, I send him and commend him to Your Reverence, who will be to him a more helpful father than I can be. I have nothing here to add concerning the person of my son. I merely say that I am giving into Your Reverence's hands the most precious thing that I possess in all the world, and my chiefest hope, that I placed entirely in him, of maintaining and giving glory to my family. . . .[6]

The day before, after two months of negotiations difficult for him to tolerate, Aloysius had formally renounced and distributed all his possessions, had disposed of any and all temporal goods that might accrue to him in his Jesuit years. For the first time in his Gonzaga existence, Aloysius felt utterly free.

To understand Aloysius, you must have the imagination to go back four centuries in time, to envision a teenager of remarkable intellectual, emotional, and diplomatic gifts, a young prince born to political power, confronting a decision of uncommon importance not only to himself but to his family and his countrymen — and this in the face of attractions and seductions potent enough to weaken the will of a much more mature man. He could have become the most significant figure in the Gonzaga dynasty, could have exercised unparalleled human and Christian influence on the social, political, and economic life of his time. Had he moved in this direction, hardly anyone would have faulted him. When a distinguished English Jesuit littérateur describes him as "a man who had taken all the hereditary force of [the Gonzaga] family, and had turned it full against what they had always used it for — self-enrichment; self-aggrandizement; self-worship,"[7] we should remember that Aloysius could have (and surely would have) reversed the Gonzaga "self" even if he had yielded to his father's pressures and inherited his power.

A second fascinating feature of Aloysius closes his earthbound existence. 1591 was a disastrous year for Italy. "Scarcity had become famine, and famine bred the plague. From the blackened country districts, pitiable caravans of starving peasants poured into Rome, already congested with its own population, that festered in its tortuous streets."[8] Hospitals were jammed to overflowing; men and women were dying in the streets. Superiors gave Aloysius permission to minister to the sick and dying — a reluctant permission, for his precarious health was of concern to them. Little reluctance in Aloysius. With intense joy he put the sick to bed, undressed them, washed and fed them — in fact, gave his time and effort to the most repulsive of the patients.

There is a tradition to the effect that Aloysius contracted a fatal infection, possibly from the poor fellow a famous statue represents as carried on his shoulders. An attractive tradition, but the evidence for this is slim at best. More likely, sheer exhaustion, intensified by his unremitting service of the plague-stricken, took a final toll on a flesh far from robust.[9] We are told that, as his illness moved rapidly into its last phases, one of the cardinals who frequented his bedside, Scipio Gonzaga, remarked, "He is the happiest man of all the Gonzagas."[10] During the night of June 20-21, 1591, as the octave of Corpus Christi drew to its close, Aloysius returned to his God.

Those who read Aloysius too rapidly risk sensing something of a "death wish" in his brief Jesuit existence. More than a year before his death, while at prayer, Aloysius felt suddenly convinced that he had but a short time left to live, and that, in consequence, he had to break whatever attachments still linked him to this earth. And in the early days of his illness, when a fever baffled his doctors, he wrote to his mother:

> The doctors do not know how it will finish and are trying to find remedies for my bodily health; but I find joy in thinking that God our Lord wishes to give me a more perfect health than what the doctors can give, and so things are going very cheerfully for me, with the hope of being called by God our Lord in a few months from the land of the dead to that of the living. . .[11]

No doubt, Aloysius yearned to be joined to his Lord — and that quite quickly. But his attitude is more nuanced than "death no matter what." It is more akin to Saint Paul's "To me to live is Christ, and to die is gain. If it is to be life in the flesh, that means fruitful labor for me. Yet which I shall choose I cannot tell. I am hard pressed between the two. My desire is to depart and be with Christ, for that is far better. But to remain in the flesh is more necessary on your account" (Phil 1:21-24).

I am reminded of a revealing conversation between Saint Ignatius Loyola and one of his first companions, James Laínez:

> *Ignatius*: Tell me, Master Laínez, what do you think you would do, were God our Lord to say: "If you want to die soon, I will release you from the prison of this body and give you eternal glory. If you prefer to stay alive, I give you no assurance as to what will become of you. . . ." If our Lord told you this, and you thought that by remaining for some time in this life you could render some outstanding service to His Divine Majesty, which would you choose?
> *Laínez*: I must confess, Father, I would choose to go soon to enjoy God and to assure my salvation and to avoid the perils in so important a matter.
> *Ignatius*: I certainly would not. If I thought that by remaining in this life I could render some signal service to our Lord, I would beg him to leave me here until I had done it, and I would not think twice of the peril to me or the assurance of my salvation.[12]

The alternatives were never presented to Aloysius. Had he been given a simple choice — enjoyment of God in heaven or enjoyment of God on earth — he would surely have opted for the former. But had God just suggested tarrying awhile in order to "render some outstanding service to His Divine Majesty," I believe his response would have echoed that of Ignatius. I say this in the light of his general attitude of Ignatian "indifference," the crucial thesis in the *Spiritual Exercises* to the effect that, as far as it is left to our free choice, "we do not seek health rather than sickness, prefer wealth to poverty, honor to contempt, a long life to a short one [and vice versa]."[13] I say it, too, on the basis of an enlightening conversation Aloysius had with Father Achilles Gagliardi on prayer. The priest had concluded that Aloysius' gift of unitive prayer might conflict with a Jesuit's spirit of accessibility to others. Aloysius simply replied that if he found his prayer interfering with his service of others, he would be suspicious of it and judge it unsuitable to his Jesuit existence.[14]

Remember, too, that despite his hazardous health Aloysius kept badgering superiors to let him labor with the plague-infected. Not indeed to hasten his own death; rather because he consistently felt called there where others needed him most.

III

It is within those two facets of his life — the Gonzaga heir who surrendered it all, and the young Jesuit who gave his life for the contagious sick — that I find Aloysius a potentially powerful model for today's young men and women. To an age and a culture where wealth, power, and fame are arguably the three goals most attractive to a discouragingly large number of our young, Aloysius argues the joy of poverty, powerlessness, and obscurity in the image of Christ. Not for their own sake. Wealth, power, and fame are not evils in themselves; to be poor, powerless, or obscure is not automatically to be ethically good or holy. Their significance lies in a three-letter question: Why?

Why did Aloysius surrender his inheritance, give up unconditionally the possibility of power, opt for the hidden life of the young Christ? Very simply, because he was convinced that it was God who was calling him to such surrender. It was a gradual process of increasing clarity. Early on he was quite sure of only one thing: a life

31

under the three religious vows. "It was the transitoriness of what most men seek that impressed him. The struggle for honors seemed to him quite mad; and the methods of wringing wealth from the poor, wicked."[15] But he still had to choose among three types of religious orders: the primarily contemplative, the primarily active, and the mixed or apostolic. Why did he decide on "contemplation in action," specifically on the Society of Jesus? (1) The Society was still young, in its first fervor. (2) It excluded ecclesiastical preferments by a special vow. (3) It focused especially on the education of youth. (4) He was attracted by the Society's missionary successes in the Indies and Japan.[16]

I do not believe Aloysius was blind to the good he could effect as a secular prince, to the untold thousands whose life he could make more human as a singular type of Gonzaga. Nor was he blind to what a Charles Borromeo was able to do for the underprivileged as a prince of the Church. Above all these considerations was a single overriding fact: God was calling him elsewhere, to vowed life in the Society of Jesus. It was as simple as that. *God* was calling. Not human reasoning; not objective argument. Simply, God.

It is often argued that the cultural climate in contemporary America makes a religious vocation, or even high sanctity, less of an option for the young, that what sociologist Robert Bellah called a resurgence of late-nineteenth-century rugged individualism is hostile to the sacrifice that sanctity demands. A seductive thesis — till you recapture the culture that produced an Aloysius, recall the Gonzaga genes, relive the bloody background that went into his fashioning. Priesthood and sisterhood have indeed turned less attractive; seminaries and convents are often "bare ruined choirs." But the urge to give all to God, especially in service to God's crucified images, is not dead or even moribund. Despite overhanging student loans, Georgetown grads pack off to the poor in Peru; join the Jesuit Volunteers here, in Belize, in Nepal, in Micronesia; serve the scarred, pimped, angel-dusted runaway youngsters in Covenant Houses across the country. God still calls, and the young still respond.

I doubt that Aloysius sparks any of these vocations. Perhaps it is unrealistic and wishful to dream that he could. But we will never know unless we actually try Aloysius on the young, present him in his

Gonzagan reality, portray him not as a bloodless, effeminate, pietistic statue but as he described himself, "a piece of twisted iron" who "entered religion to get twisted straight,"[17] the Aloysius who loved the dying so intensely that he yearned to die for and with them — and did. Unfortunately, the saints do not share in our American Catholic life the way they did in mid-century — not in our schooling, not in our liturgy, not in our private prayer.

Today's idols are the entertainers, the athletes, and the men and women who make it big in business: Tom Cruise and Madonna, Joe Montana and Martina Navratilova, Lee Iacocca and Gloria Steinem. It may well be that only the living inspire imitation, that the dead are, well, dead. But within Catholicism it will always be a tragedy when the "communion of saints" in the present no longer includes the heroes of the past; when names like Augustine and Aquinas, Catherine of Siena and Teresa of Ávila, Ignatius Loyola and Aloysius Gonzaga, Thomas Merton and Dorothy Day are no longer in our vocabulary; when men and women who reflected Christ in so many different and astonishing ways are no longer our pathfinders.

Can we reach God without them? Of course. After all, Saint Peter's words in first-century Jerusalem are no less true today: "There is no other name under heaven . . . by which we must be saved" (Acts 4:12). No other name save Jesus. A Christian's ultimate model is always and everywhere the Christ whose grace enables Christian holiness. Still, an Aloysius patterned after Christ can reveal in real life what the Gospels do not disclose about Christ: how sanctity works itself out for the adolescent and the young adult. Such an example can be particularly potent in an affluent culture because it shows how sacrifice of status and of life itself once graced a Gonzaga born with a silver spoon in his mouth.

Total gift of self to God, utter self-giving to the "least" of Christ's brothers and sisters — Aloysius flings a strong but attractive challenge to today's young. I refuse to censure the young for not responding to him; they have never been confronted with him. We Jesuits who feasted on him as novices rarely carried him with us as we "matured" in the Society. Our heroes were the explorers — Ignatius braving Rome and Xavier baptizing India, Ricci mesmerizing mandarins and Bobola butchered by Ukrainian Cossacks, Campion challenging

33

England's Privy Council with his bravura "Brag" and Jogues mutilated by the Iroquois in New York. Must we wait for a Pop recording by, say, New Kids on the Block if Aloysius Gonzaga is to come alive again? Or the type of biography that John F. Kennedy inspired, he too cut down in his prime: William Manchester's *One Brief Shining Moment*, Arthur Schlesinger's *A Thousand Days*, or Kenneth O'Donnell's *Johnny, We Hardly Knew Ye*?

Yes, we hardly knew him, hardly know him, this Prince Aluigi who gave up all for God — all save the images of God for whom he gave his life. Cannot a Catholic imagination resurrect him after four centuries, bring him to life for a generation of youth captivated by exciting role models?

NOTES

1. Karl Rahner, "Following the Crucified," *Theological Investigations* 18: *God and Revelation* (New York: Crossroad, 1983) 157-170, at 165-166.

2. I attempted to exemplify this thesis in a book published twenty-six years ago, *Saints and Sanctity* (Englewood Cliffs, N.J.: Prentice-Hall. 1965); it contains sermons and addresses on twenty saints. The thesis as enunciated above is taken in large measure from the Preface of that volume (pp. v-vii).

3. Desmond Reid, S.J., "St. Aloysius Gonzaga, Patron of Youth," in Robert Nash, S.J., ed., *Jesuits: Biographical Essays* (Westminster, Md.: Newman, 1956), 25-35, at 25.

4. Ibid., 26.

5. Ibid., 72.

6. Translation as in C. C. Martindale, S.J., *The Vocation of Aloysius Gonzaga* (New York: Sheed and Ward, 1945) 128-129.

7. Martindale, ibid., 132.

8. Ibid., 217.

9. See P. Molinari, S.J., "St. Aloysius Gonzaga, " in *Companions of Jesus: Spiritual Profiles of the Jesuit Saints and Beati* (2nd ed. Rome: Gregorian University, 1984), 73: "In spite of his labors for the plague-stricken poor, whom he visited and nursed in their homes,

Aloysius did not catch the disease. All the same, he died on 21 June, 1591 after a short period of rapidly increasing exhaustion. It was his self-dedication that killed him, his love that drove him to respond to the cries of pain, that is, to the call of Christ who in his suffering brethren needs comfort and loving care: 'What you did to one of the least of these my brethren, you did to me' (Matt. 25:40)" (emphasis mine).

10. Quoted in Martindale, *Vocation,* op. cit., 222.

11. Quoted ibid., 224.

12. Pedro Rivadeneira, *Vida del bienaventurado Padre Ignacio de Loyola* (2nd ed.; Barcelona: Subirana, 1885), 501-502.

13. From the "Principle and Foundation" of the *Spiritual Exercises of St. Ignatius.*

14. See Martindale, *Vocation,* 198.

15. Ibid., 73.

16. Here I am indebted to Maurice Meschler, S.J., *Life of St. Aloysius Gonzaga, Patron of Christian Youth* (St. Louis: Herder, 1911), 79.

17. Quoted from Martindale, *Vocation* [1].

"St. Aloysius Gonzaga with Abused Children" by William Hart McNichols

III

Saint Aloysius: Patron of Youth

William Hart McNichols, S.J.

"The Lord nurtured and taught him; he guarded him as the apple of his eye . . . the Lord alone was his leader."
                                        Deuteronomy 32:10-12

S ome years ago, I was visiting my parent's home in Colorado when I decided to look through a drawer of *Jesuit Bulletins* my mother keeps faithfully in a living room table. I was actually looking for a picture of my then favorite Jesuit saint, the English poet/martyr Saint Robert Southwell. Instead I stumbled across a June issue with a photograph of a sculpture of Saint Aloysius Gonzaga, by the sculptor Pierre Legros (1666-1719).

Images have always had a great power over me, and for a long time, I didn't understand why. Practically everything I first knew of my faith was mediated through music and art. At times these creations were also purveyors of hope because the art attested to a spiritual world so vivid, so confrontational and glorious, that it partially healed the great sense of separation and longing I felt. I think so many children begin their relationships with those friends of heaven in this way. And though there might be suspicion and misunderstanding concerning this attitude toward images in Western Christianity, in the Eastern churches there has always been this deep reverence for icons. The painting of an icon is a painstakingly prayerful labor of love. Those who do this work, as well as those who receive it, believe the icon "holds" the presence of the one it portrays. In this tradition, the presence is restricted to icons, but I imagine countless numbers of people have encountered the spiritual world in classical works, primitive and folk works, and even the most simple and critically condemned "kitsch" art.

The day I saw the Legros sculpture of Aloysius really began my relationship with him. I brought the magazine back to New York and had the photograph enlarged for the wall of my room. For many months I don't remember reading anything about him at all; I just kept visiting the picture. Gradually something of Aloysius began to come to me. Because of Pope Benedict XIII's appointment of him as the patron of youth in 1729, Aloysius is the most visible and well-known of all the Jesuit saints. Also, according to nearly every article or book you read, he is the most apologized-for and defended Jesuit saint. People are strongly divided over Aloysius, he has been called the "saint's saint," an "impossible prig," "a child prodigy," and in his own time, as a page at the court of Philip II of Spain, "not of flesh and blood" . . . an angel in human form. But Legros's sculpture has none of the familiar poses and symbols which may have contributed to his loss of friends over the years. There are no crowns, lilies, books, crosses or altar boy's attire, and perhaps it was actually the absence of these accumulated props which let me finally meet the boy of radiant inner strength and infinite tenderness sculpted by Legros. Even now, after some time with the image, it almost hurts to see Aloysius trying to lift a man who seems twice his age and weight, yet the boy's expression is focused and careful. The man he carries looks both sick and rested — the gesture of his head and the expression on his face "speak" a trust and safety of a child at home in the arms of a parent. This alone said, and says, worlds and worlds about Aloysius Gonzaga. It also echoes something of the biblical prophecy of the "leading child" and the reversal of roles Jesus promised in the Sermon on the Mount and parables of the kingdom of God.

The facts about Aloysius' life came in slowly, after attention to the Legros sculpture. Some of them surprised me, some shocked me, some made me laugh, and made me want to kneel down like Saint Peter before the Lord, awed by the great ocean of mercy present in such a being of holiness. The best short account can be found in the June volume of *Butler's Lives of the Saints*, and there are three biographies considered to be great by Jesuits: one by Father Cepari (a contemporary of Aloysius) and two later works by Father Martindale and Father Meschler; the Meschler is still in print through TAN publishers, and the other two can be hunted down in libraries.

Briefly, Aloysius was born into the old and powerful Gonzaga dynasty, March 9, 1568, in the family castle near Mantua, in the town of Castiglione delle Stiviere. The more one learns about the Gonzagas, the more extraordinary Aloysius seems. Though the Gonzaga family had no corner on high Renaissance ruthlessness and evil, by modern standards they make cardboard villains out of figures on daytime television and put the sagas of "Dallas" and "Dynasty" to shame. Soon after the death of Aloysius, his brother Ridolfo was murdered and later his mother was nearly stabbed to death, but was restored to health, she believed, by Aloysius' intercession. In the recent best seller, *A Renaissance Tapestry: The Gonzaga of Mantua*, author Kate Simon fleshes out a family portrait very rich in detail and scholarship. In chapter two, Simon states that it was quite common for women to abuse little boys at the great banquets and dances. I remember virtually every biographer of Aloysius trying in vain to explain his extreme anti-social behavior at these events, and especially his legendary "modesty of the eyes." If he wasn't actually abused himself, he was certainly aware of it, and sometimes the only power a child may have, given this kind of an assault from an adult, is to flee or avert his or her eyes. Having been given the grace of chastity at the age of nine, little Aloysius was aggressively conscious of guarding this miraculous gift. These tales of his vigilant self-protection, and Simon's account of regular child abuse, led me to "add a wing" onto Aloysius' title of patron of youth, and to place all abused children in his arms. These incidents are so widespread and common now that we need an intercessor who is strong, who understand the complications of this wounding, and who holds in his arms the soothing balm, offering us this light of healing.

Aloysius had to fight a long and bloody battle with his father, Ferrante, to get his permission to renounce the Marquisate of Castiglione, as rightful heir, and let it fall to his younger brother Ridolfo, in order for him to enter the Society of Jesus. Ferrante appears, in these times of struggle, very much the formidable opponent and nearly the match for the strength of Aloysius. He was given to frightening fits of rage and was a compulsive gambler. On the other side, he truly loved and admired Aloysius, and was all too aware of the boy's ambassadorial sophistication and solid "businesslike" skills. Later on in the novitiate, the other novices would pick this up quickly, and nicknamed him "*generalino*" — sure that as an adult he would be general of the order. Ferrante knew that if Aloysius yielded his title, none of the other children was capable of carrying on the family business and "reputation." Ironically, Aloysius actually cleansed and glorified the Gonzaga name beyond anyone's imagining. It seems amazing now that Ferrante did not see what everyone saw so clearly in his son: a full-grown sage and saint in a child's body, much the same way the little Mozart held a full-grown genius and composer of symphonies in a child's body. Finally, Ferrante could no longer fight the concentrated single-mindedness of a boy visited, like the young King David, with the power of God. Aloysius won the contest for his own life through a flood of prayer and penances, which included taking upon himself the resistance and anger of his father, scourging these in his own body with a dog whip until he drew blood. In these disciplines at prayer and sustained asceticism, he often reminds me of the Buddha, another holy young prince who left the splendid life and palace of his family, and poured himself into meditation and severe asceticism after encountering the vast suffering of people in the "outside" world. And it's true, there is something pale and opalescent, like the light of the moon, in these two souls; both reflect another light, and both have a shining serenity which seems to rise and light the night of suffering.

If it can be said that each of us has a mission, which can be detected in seed from our earliest years, and then, like the refrain of a song, is played over and over again, no matter the length of time in our lives or the myriad situations — then it can be said that Aloysius was much the same in the Jesuits as he had been all through his childhood. Within the Society of Jesus he astonished people with his spiritual maturity, again . . . as if an aged desert father had come to inhabit a teenaged boy. The paradox is, both were present in him; he was graced beyond his years, and he was young and loved and attractive to the young. This comes through very strongly in the stories of his period of teaching, where students gathered around Aloysius quite naturally and were led by him into an enduring relationship with God. He was loved and revered too by the Jesuits. His spiritual director, Saint Robert Bellarmine, was constantly quoting Aloysius' insights into the contemplative life to the young Jesuits. Bellarmine marveled at his holiness, and he was the priest brought to anoint Aloysius on his deathbed. He also begged to be buried at the feet of his "spiritual child," and this was granted to him; he is buried near the body of Aloysius, in St. Ignatius Church in Rome.

In 1591, a vicious plague ravaged Rome. The Jesuits opened a hospital in the city, and the provincial and the general worked with the dying. Many Jesuits also caught the plague and died; Aloysius was one of the many, recovering briefly according to Butler, and it is said he caught the plague from one last dying man he just had to carry in off the streets . . . this is the glorious moment depicted by Legros.

And this final work of Aloysius has again led me to add yet another wing to his patronage of youth; this time asking him to embrace all the men, women, youth, and children who are suffering from AIDS. For many years, as I have been privileged to work with people with AIDS, I have seen him at work. He brings a gentle brotherhood to the young who find him so comforting, and he brings his love of the Blessed Mother, her way of mercy, and her way of prayer.

It would take another whole article for me to recount the miraculous blessings and great healings Aloysius has brought to people with AIDS, so let me sum them up and end this story with a prayer written for the sick and suffering:

> Aloysius,
> You have drawn me to you, gentle teacher, loving guide. I am filled with gratitude to you . . . I love you. Just to see you, to sit with your image, is to see all the simplicity, the trust, and the innocence of the children of the kingdom.
> Aloysius,
> Let me serve, let me love as you loved people on earth! Teach me to leave the dark destructive forces within for the Light in the presence of Our Savior, Jesus.
> Aloysius,
> Teach me to pray unceasingly: better yet, pray with me, sit near me, kneel with me . . . take my hand. And finally, when my life here is over, come to lead me Home.
> Amen.

IV

On Reading the Life of Saint Aloysius Gonzaga: Reflections on Saints and Saints' Lives[1]

Wendy M. Wright

U gh, Mom! You're reading one of those old mildewed things again," exclaimed my twelve-year-old daughter as she gingerly fingered the frayed binding of my library book with her newly polished nails. "They all smell bad, and they're always about those really weird guys who lived so long ago."

"You've looked at it," I ventured.

"Yeah, but it was really bizarre. Why don't you join the twentieth century, Mom?" she called back as she swept out of the door into the sunlight of twentieth-century America and left me to the dark specters of the sixteenth-century Italian renaissance.

She had raised the question, albeit somewhat frivolously, that I have been asking myself for a good number of years. Why, or rather how, does one read saints' lives? The traditional answer, given by religious persons with what today would be called "pastoral concerns," would have been "For edification." One reads the lives of the saints to be inspired in the ideals of the Christian faith, seeing in the lives of heroic men and women the wondrous movements of grace coating the God-directed potential of humankind into activity. Thus one might be moved to admire or even emulate the life of "perfection" that the saints reveal, as did the illustrious Cardinal Bellarmine, Aloysius Gonzaga's Jesuit confessor, when he posthumously reported on the purity and freedom from mortal sin that he had observed in his younger contemporary.

"I believe that he went straight to Heaven, and I have always scrupled to pray to God for the repose of his soul for it seemed to me that this would underrate the graces of God which I had seen in him."[2]

Similarly, one might read a saint's life to be taught that God's power continues to be channeled through the holy ones of the Church and to be either comforted or amazed that healing and special graces might be obtained through the intercession of persons like Saint Aloysius. Certainly the intense focus in much hagiographical writing is upon the wonder-working or intercessory power of the saints. In a late-nineteenth-century life of Aloysius, a considerable portion of the book is dedicated to describing the cult of the youthful Gonzaga and to documenting evidence of the miraculous healings ascribed to his intercession.[3]

Or if one reads with more academic intent, one might read saints' lives to uncover patterns or "styles" of sanctity that reveal the religious and/or cultural sensibilities of an age. From this perspective, Aloysius' intense self-crucifying spirituality might well be observed against the backdrop of the contemporary discussions of late medieval spirituality as it uncovers the basic pattern of imitation of Christ as redemptive participatory suffering.[4] Or one might look for indications of a culture's sensibilities about childhood or the body or any number of topics.[5] And if one were of a more serious theological bent, one might consult the saints to cull out their unique insights into the nature of God and the Christian mysteries in order to do constructive theology.[6]

But none of these approaches is the one I want to take here. I do not want to see Saint Aloysius as an interesting historic figure frozen in the antique landscape of sanctity. Nor do I wish to edify, to simply rehearse the arguments for the perfection of his life or his intercessory and wonder-working capacities. Rather, I would like to reframe the entire endeavor of reading a saint's life, and to do that by considering what we, as contemporary readers, presently look for in such a life and for what we might search further. I would like to reflect critically on what might be gained by reading a saint's life, especially one like the life of Aloysius Gonzaga, an Italian renaissance prince who rejected both the luxury and sinister decadence of his patrimony in favor of an austere, almost driven life as a member of the vigorous young Society of Jesus, and who died at the age of twenty-three.

As a scholar of religion, a middle class American woman with feminist interests, a wife and mother who has lived into the burdens and perspectives of middle age, my personal relationship to Saint Aloysius, beyond sheer historical curiosity, would seem to be a tenuous one. True, as has been pointed out, the youthful aristocrat might be seen as an impressive Christian witness to a materialistic and relativistic culture.[7] One has only to read the accounts of the atmosphere of continual familial and political violence in which he was raised to gain some sympathy for the revulsion he seemed to feel for "the world."[8] And one has only to tap into one's own religious instincts that yearn to simplify in the midst of superfluousness and to be still in the center of a tense, overstimulating culture to identify with the sensitive young man's embrace of the evangelical counsels in his Jesuit vows. Any quest to secure personal dignity and integrity in the context of a culture which degrades and dehumanizes is a story that could be considered meaningful today.

But there is much about Aloysius that might tend to deflect the modern reader (beyond the mustiness of the volumes that have sat on the back shelves of seminary and retreat-house libraries). For Aloysius' severe asceticism and his uncompromising, even self-destructive pursuit of religious virtue is foreign to our sensibilities. This is true even if we comprehend the context of both the spirituality of his era (with its literal affective identification with the crucified Christ) and his own family history (with its legacy of startling brutality against the backdrop of which a life of personal purity must have been a welcome release). Further, the fact that he is a man, a very young one at that, and a saint whose story seems to rehearse the all-too-familiar, other worldly, anti-body sanctity scenario being discarded or at least reviewed with skepticism these days, removes him one step further from our lives.[9] He is a figure not readily accessible to the modern reader, especially if we are reading his life (and saints' lives in general) as models to live by.

Saints as Models

And that is precisely what many contemporary Catholics seem to be doing today. We are no longer interested in reading about men and women whose superhuman exploits fill us with awe and cause us to tremble at the divine touch. In our post-Freudian age, we aren't much enamored with perfection as a description of mature personal authenticity. Nor do we relate to the saints very comfortably as intermediaries or loci of spiritual power who can act as either bridges for our prayers or as channels for healing or miracle-working. Our world is the global village, not the hierarchical chain of being of a bygone age.

Theologian Lawrence Cunningham in his book *The Meaning of Saints*[10] argues quite persuasively that this exemplary or modeling function of the saints is what is most needed in our tradition today. He traces the history of sanctity from the martyrs to the confessors of the fourth through sixth centuries, describing the evolution of a distinctive type of saint whose life was a mixture of asceticism and miracle-working. The best example of this genre is *The Life of Martin of Tours*, written by Sulpicius Severus around the turn of the fifth century, which became a model for all later hagiography.[11] The emphasis on the miraculous, which Cunningham sees as central to the identity of early Christendom in its efforts to overthrow the powers of "pagan" deities, continued as a primary characteristic of saints' lives throughout the middle ages. This emphasis, which greatly overshadowed the exemplary value of such lives, continues to this day to be institutionalized by the Church in the process of canonization, which requires serious evidence of miraculous occurrence as part of its formal procedure.[12] What this produces, Cunningham argues, is a pantheon of holy ones venerated for reasons that are outside the experience and concerns of the average Christian. Models of the deeply lived Christian life are what we need, models that reveal the possibility of transparent goodness, encompassing charity, mastery of self, the absorption of the Christ event into human life and the mystery of God's grace active in the world. We need models, not wonder-workers.

Other contemporary scholars and theologians echo similar concerns. In a book of sermons entitled *Saints and Sanctity* published two decades ago, Walter Burghardt anticipated Cunningham's concerns about the significance of yesterday's saint for today's Christian.[13] Burghardt suggests steering a middle road between the extremes of viewing saints' lives as normative (slavish imitation) or as irrelevant to contemporary

Christendom, worthy of reverence but not of serious examination for the Christian life today. Rather, he sees in the lives of yesterday's saints illustrations of "certain principles or facts of Christian spirituality that are permanently valid, that have a relevance transcending persons and places, eras and situations."[14] They can exemplify the enduring values of solitude, renewal, conversion, the religious quest and so forth. While Burghardt does not critique the process that raises up certain persons and features of their lives (i.e., wonder-working) for communal emulation as Cunningham does, he does nonetheless focus on the exemplary aspect of saints' lives. They are there for us as models.

Similarly, revisionist theologian Shawn Madigan in an unpublished dissertation from Catholic University raises the question of canonized saints and their function within today's worshiping communities.[15] Arguing for the need for a more radical revamping of the liturgical calendar than was carried out during Vatican II, Madigan claims that paradigm shifts in modern Christology and ecclesiology necessitate the reconsideration of the *models* of holiness presently dominating the calendar to more clearly reflect the universality (in terms of geography, chronology, and significance) of those whose lives share in the fullness of the paschal mystery and model the Christ-life for the entire Church. While Madigan's emphasis is on the need for revision in the calendar to reflect contemporary theological shifts, the assumption is clearly made that the saints and their lives function for us today as models.

Even the more popular literature reflects this idea that the saints serve us primarily in this exemplary way. Nowhere can this be seen more clearly than in the recent popular "naming" of contemporary religious figures such as Mother Teresa, Dorothy Day, Oscar Romero, and others as saints. Inevitably it is the qualities or actions of these persons — in these cases, their deep identification with the poor and suffering — that singles them out for attention.[16] All this is indicative of a post-Vatican II reorientation in the way the saints and the living are seen to interrelate. Elizabeth Johnson has put it well:

A basic shift has occurred . . . because of the Council's emphasis on companionship. In the centuries after Trent . . . the saints, including

Mary, were thought to be mediators in the sense that they came between Jesus Christ and believers, even while being subordinated to him . . . from the sixteenth to the twentieth centuries . . . veneration of the saints took the predominant form of a patron-petitioner model . . . The effect of conciliar teachings has been to shift the basic model to one of communion and solidarity. . . . Saints are comrades, fellow disciples, pilgrims with us who follow after the one love . . . the relationship between all of the redeemed is fundamentally collegial.[17]

All of these contemporary Catholic voices, as diverse as their interests in reevaluating the meaning of saints might be, do speak with one voice on this one theme: the saints are important primarily because they function as models for a well-lived Christian life.

This means that the older ways of envisioning the importance of saints seem no longer to work for us. Gone is the Greco-Roman thought world in which patron spirits populated the Mediterranean basin and served as protecting presences. Gone thus are the patron saints that replaced them. Virtually gone is the (to many of us) ancient mentality in which the tombs and relics of those recognized as having been holy served as gathering places for the Christian community. Gone is the sense of divine energy being manifested in those bones and shrines.[18]

Diminished too is the hierarchical medieval universe in which saints and angels formed the rungs of an ascending ladder of being reaching toward the divine eternal and spiritual reality. Gone thus is our sense of intermediary beings, presences that can assist us in our endeavors or bring us messages from the divine realm. Eroded as well is our sense of the dead as being with us, as being present and active in our lives.[19]

If, as these varied voices suggest, our basic Christian world view, our ecclesiology, and our Christology have moved away from bygone patronal and hierarchical models; if we now see church primarily as a community of adult mutuality and companionship; if Jesus —the source of all holiness — is less head of the body than our brother, where does that leave the saints?[20] They then are companions, human beings whose life choices and actions have made them models of transparent goodness and encompassing charity.

I must admit that I am among those whose basic sensibilities in these matters are frankly American and feminist. An image of church and the saints which smacks too much of the undemocratic, patriarchal images of bygone eras troubles me. Unquestioning obedience to any authority that has not been delegated by communal consent as well as subordination to a male-dominated power structure whose perspectives reflect mainly the privileged experience of the few, are issues that cause me some difficulty. From this perspective, the elitism of both Aloysius Gonzaga's life as Renaissance prince and as cleric alienate his life from mine. And his wonder-working, his power of intercession, is this not simply a reinforcement of the hierarchical structure through which divine power and grace itself was, in the now-challenged model of church, supposed to flow? Do I need Aloysius as mediator any longer? If he is stripped of this function, how do I find him as a model? The difficulty of doing this has been suggested above. If the saints are going to be good models, unless I really want to abstract out certain characteristics that I wish to emulate (like Aloysius' cultural resistance, which, I'll have to admit, is pretty impressive), then I'll need models that fit my life circumstances more closely. I'll need more women saints, and married women at that, noted for their holiness, not in spite of or after the death of their spouses and children, but precisely because of their holiness lived, not "perfectly" but authentically, in the midst of diapers, adolescent rebellion, mortgages, menopause and the tedium of sustaining life-giving relationships.[21] I'll need saints that recognize sin as structural and societal and not just personal, saints who struggle to right injustice and to educate themselves as peacemakers. I'll need very "human" saints, not paragons of supernatural virtue but individuals whose struggles seem close to mine. For models and companions, if they are going to be at all meaningful, must walk a path I too can walk.

As I have suggested, this seems to be the consensus of much of today's Catholic community.

"The saints are with their sisters and brothers in the one community
. . . gratitude and delight in the cloud of witnesses with whom we
share a common humanity and a common faith commend their
memory to our interest."[22]

The Communion of Saints

Of all this revitalized and reconstructed thinking about the
saints, I am aware and supportive. Yet what is missing? Why don't
I put down my *Life of Aloysius* once and for all and follow my
daughter out the door into the sunlight of the twentieth century in
search of new, meaningful models of sanctity? What is there woven
into the fabric of this life that keeps me seated in my chair turning
those musty pages? Beyond the fact that I simply find history
fascinating, it has, I think, something to do with the word
communion.

When there is a liturgical occasion on which we recite the
Apostles' Creed, we find ourselves professing our belief in, among
other things, the "holy catholic church, the communion of saints." The
phrase "communion of saints" seems to have first appeared in one
version of the creed at the end of the fourth century and then come
into general use in the Roman Church by the sixth.[23] The meaning of
the cryptic phrase is debated among theologians of different
denominations, but in Catholic circles the phrase has a particular and
distinctive feel to it.[24] Technically it is linked with the idea of the three
states of the Church: the Church militant, suffering, and triumphant (to
use the traditional terminology) or the church in pilgrimage (on earth),
in purification (in purgatory), and in glory (in heaven). It is also
connected to the uniquely, among Christian denominations, Roman
and Anglo-Catholic sensibility that there is some sort of vital
interconnection between the Christians in each of these states.[25] The
awareness of this interconnection is expressed through the veneration
of those members of the Church somehow already thought a part of
the Church in heaven, and in the intercession which those members
provide for other members of the Church. Thus there are felt to be
special holy persons, especially among those who have died, who
show forth the radiance of the Christ-life shared by all Christians
through baptism, in a recognizably unique way. And the depth and

fullness of the holiness they radiate is available somehow and spills over refreshing and replenishing the Church as a whole.

While this is only a partial exploration of the doctrine of the communion of saints, it is a fairly accurate account of the sensibility that Catholics traditionally have integrated into their sense of reality.[26] Today, however, it remains a rather tenuous notion for some. And in many post-Vatican II Catholics, it seems to be associated mainly with the devotion handed down by a grandmother or with a personal, albeit unexamined, sense of interconnection between the exemplary saints and self, a connection rarely publicly admitted.[27]

This certainly is a very foreign notion to most Protestant Christians, whose understanding of the communion of saints is of the assembly of all believers. In accordance with New Testament usage, the saints are all those who constitute the community. The sensibility among most Protestants is that those who have died, while heroic witnesses to the faith in the sense that they have proclaimed the word in their lifetimes in a special way, are not considered to be in any special relation to the living.[28] The difference in Catholic and Protestant sensibilities in this regard is most striking. It has to do with distinctive world views, predispositions in the way God, Christ, and the human person are understood. David Tracy has described this well as the Catholic "analogical imagination" in contrast to the Protestant "dialectical imagination."[29] To reduce a complex analysis to rather simple terms, Tracy sees that Catholicism tends to emphasize the similarity between God and objects, events, experiences, and persons in the natural world, while the Protestant (and, incidentally, Islamic and Jewish) religious imaginations tend to emphasize the difference between God and the world. The former stresses the continuity and similarity between the sacred and the human and created realm while the latter stresses their radical discontinuity.[30]

The place of the saint in either imaginative construct must also differ. In the traditional Catholic view, the human person somehow actually participates, to a greater or lesser degree, in the divine life itself. Persons can be like, or can image, God. Saints are those persons whose participation or likeness is of a greater degree.

This is a rankling notion to a dialectical imagination, which would recoil at the suggestion that anything or anyone in the created realm might be "closer to" or "more like" the divine, which remains one, utterly unique, unlike all others and ultimately unnameable. The saints in this view are simply the members of the Church, baptized through the grace of God into the redeeming life of Christ whose gift is neither merited nor obtained in differing degrees.

Beyond this imaginative capacity there are also good historical reasons why the traditional Catholic notion of saints was rejected in the Reformation. Specifically, the sale of indulgences — the transfer of the excess merits of the saints that were thought to belong to the Church to the benefit of other Christians, living or dead, whose virtues were deficient — had become a mercantile venture. Abuse that had political and economic motives was rampant. The sense of who the saints were and especially of how their holiness was to be regarded had sadly degenerated, along with much else in the late medieval church. A rather mechanical, mercantile model of grace as dispensed through ecclesial channels (and through the saints as functionaries) needed correction. The Reformation certainly did that. But, I would suggest, some of the richness and vitality of insight that lay buried behind the indulgence travesty was abandoned in the wake of reforming zeal.

The notion of a special function of saints did remain in the Tridentine Catholic synthesis and was cleansed of much of its most flagrant abuse. But it became so closely linked to the hierarchical ecclesial model, and to the clerical prerogatives championed by militant Catholicism of the late sixteenth through mid-twentieth century, that it became virtually inseparable from them.[31]

So perhaps it is not surprising that in the late twentieth century in those elements of the post-Vatican II American Catholic Church which are strongly "Protestantized" in the sense of stressing egalitarian models of ministry and church organization, an interest in saints has either been lost or interest is focused on highlighting their exemplary function alone. Likewise not surprising is the fact that the more traditional elements of that same Church (which cling to the hierarchical church model, stress guidance from above and the unique power of designated authority) retain a lively interest in saints as intercessors and wonder-workers as well as models, and have claimed the prerogative to use the term "communion" (which comes directly from the credal statement about saints) to be the byword that best expresses their entire religious perspective.[32]

Reevaluating the Communion of Saints

While I do not wish to pit segments of the American Catholic Church against one another (it is hoped that they are part of one community whose theological perspectives slide along one broad symbolic continuum), I do think it is important to recognize to what extent present notions of sanctity are bound up with a wider range of disputed ecclesial images. What I would hope to do is loosen that binding a bit and, drawing upon the wisdom of both sides of the spectrum of contemporary Catholic thought, imaginatively turn the idea of the communion of saints about and look at it anew.

The germ of the notion of the communion of saints is found mainly in the Pauline texts of the New Testament. Indeed, traditional Catholic commentators looking for biblical sources for the mature doctrine have looked first to those passages in Paul.[33] For while he certainly never speaks of "communion" (nor is there evidence of anyone doing so before the fourth century) and while he refers to all the faithful as "saints" (e.g. 1 Cor. 1:1-3), he also sees a special union among the faithful. They are saints — holy — in the sense that they share in the holiness of Christ. And they are one body with many members (Rom. 12:4-13, 1 Cor. 12:12-27) who seem to have a unique spiritual connection. The apostle acknowledges his prayer on their behalf (Rom. 1:9-10) and requests their prayers in return (Rom. 15:30-32). Further, the gifts and goods of each of the members are given precisely for the benefit of whole, one's talents and charisms supplying the lack in another's in a reciprocal way (1 Cor. 12, Rom. 12:3-8). And Paul's emphasis on the new Christ-reality born in the Christian community through the reception of the one Spirit, which inspires or breathes through each of the members, further underscores the impression that these saints in the early Christian communities are seen to relate to one another in new and radical ways never before imaginable (Eph. 4:1-8, Col. 1:24, and 2 Cor. 1:1-7).

It is not my intent here to trace the full development of the Catholic idea of the communion of the saints through the first centuries of Christian experience in detail; suffice it to say that a variety of interpretations about what the term saints really meant were extant in the early Church. As Christianity under the persecutions came to a heightened self-understanding, the idea grew up that there were those in the community who were special holy witnesses. These, the martyrs primarily, but also the apostles, were seen to manifest the holiness of Christ to a greater degree than other Christians.[34]

The martyrs were thought to participate in the redemptive death of Christ through their own dying, to proceed directly to heaven upon their deaths; to provide a link between the living and the dead, and to intercede for those on earth.[35] The writings of the church fathers and the evidence of early liturgical formulas seem to indicate the gradual evolution of a full-blown understanding of all the members of the Church, both living and dead, united with and through Christ in a vital interdependent spiritual network. While the technical understanding of the term communion of saints admitted to many variants for most of Christian history even in Catholic circles,[36] the point is that there has existed for centuries a most notable organic metaphor that empresses a deep truth about how people might think about themselves in relation to one another.

It is a countercultural metaphor today, just as it was centuries ago. It reverses the cultural norm of self-identity. Just as following Jesus during the movement's early history (and indeed much later[37]) had to do with replacing the normative ties of family and clan with the new ties of Christian commitment, so being a Christian, as suggested by the notion of communion of saints, had (and has) to do with understanding the depth of those ties which are not merely social or biological. In classic Christian thought, entry into the mystical body, through baptism, initiated one into the reality of that depth dimension.

But if the metaphor is looked at with a somewhat wider lens than the lens of classic Christian theology, it is obvious what a striking metaphor it is and how deeply it challenges our contemporary sense of reality. It suggests that we are other than our socialization would suggest we are. We are, first, not simply atomized individuals whose unique destinies only tangentially impinge on other individual lives. We are not bounded selves. Our identity is not exhausted with the enunciation of the first-person pronoun. Second, we are not simply identified by our group associations. We are not primarily Americans, black or white, professionals of some sort or other, or part of a corporate or familial entity.

We are, rather, unique, irreplaceable elements in a larger life, a life that is at once social, biological, and spiritual. We participate in that life not in the sense that we choose or do not choose to be part of it, but in that we are intrinsically and organically connected to all the other elements of that life. The life we are part of can be described as a body, the elements within it as the members, the interrelationship between the members as communion and the depth dimension of the whole as mystical. The body is the body of holiness, of the life that participates in the divine holiness itself. The members are participants in the holiness of the body. They are the saints, the holy ones.

The saints intertwine with one another like the branches of a vine drawing life and substance from the vine itself.[38] The saints constitute a community of mutual need and nourishment, who feed and are fed by one another, whose shared lack and abundance, if allowed to distribute itself, creates an organism of profound homeostasis and wholeness. This is a countercultural concept that challenges the constructs of self we live by in mainstream twentieth-century America.[39] Our excessive individualism, coupled with our enthusiasm for identifying ourselves with the particular subgroups to which we belong, doesn't give us much sympathy for seeing ourselves as in communion with others in a larger life and participating in that life in a way that transcends our own ego boundaries.[40]

Yet the notion of the communion of saints is one which might well be reevaluated and made current for our changing sensibilities. I would like to suggest that it is a radical, countercultural metaphor which resonates well with contemporary emergent concepts that, in themselves, challenge prevailing views. I speak primarily of the feminist challenge to traditional ways of thinking about self and others which is taking place in many academic fields, and of the growing consciousness of the need for a global perspective expressed in, among other movements, the environmental movement and Catholic social teaching. While this must be too brief a discussion of these and other related, far-reaching topics, I feel concern to at least bring them up in order to place our reevaluation of this traditional Catholic doctrine in current context.

The feminist movement (a diverse phenomenon its own right) has raised many questions not only about women's issues, but about hallowed notions of self-identity that have undergirded all our Western mainstream thinking.[41]

One brief example must suffice. Feminist psychologists at the Stone Center in Massachusetts have, for the last several years, been working on redefining traditional psychological constructs about the nature of the self by drawing on research done primarily with women subjects. They have developed what they call a "self-in-relation theory."[42] Questioning traditional psychology's focus on autonomy and separation as goals of mature development, they view the self as essentially social and interactive. Persons and environments which best foster the mature self-in-relation are those that encourage mutuality and empathic communication. They define empathy as a complex process which has traditionally been little understood. It is not, as thought in most clinical circles, a mysterious, primitive phenomenon in which one clearly boundaried individual fuses temporarily with another and then separates again in order not to lose self-identity. Rather, empathy is a capacity of the person (often most highly developed in women because of the culture's assignment of relational work to them) in which one emotionally experiences the world from the internal perspective of another while at the same time cognitively recognizing that the experience is not one's own. If the empathic experience remains fluid, one is moved by the other and comes to see the world through a fresh perspective.

Many scholars in diverse fields, the psychologists at the Stone Center being an example, are presently challenging classical Western norms for envisioning the self. The Stone Center's challenge is contoured by the limits of the discipline of psychology, but other fields are mounting the challenge within their own disciplines. The tremendous amount of revisionist energy in Christian theology given to integrating similar types of feminist insights indicates that our own Christian religious symbols and metaphors need to be broadened to incorporate changing views.[43]   Certainly, recent ecological sensibilities and a growing global consciousness in many other fields press us to conceive of ourselves as more inherently interdependent politically, economically, and environmentally. Likewise, contemporary Catholic social teaching rests firmly on these insights.[44] We can no longer act independently as economies or nations. The reality of our shared lives is now increasingly clear.

All of these emerging ways of thinking about ourselves, both as individuals and as societies, resonate well with the organic metaphor of the mystical body, the communion of saints. All suggest a self that can only be understood as embedded in the context of relationships. All suggest that those relationships are not peripheral to the self but essential to its very nature. They suggest that the network of selves is interdependent and mutually life-giving.

The image of humankind evoked in the traditional Catholic understanding of the communion of saints must be considered an indispensable resource for theological reflection. Once again, the self is not essentially atomistic but, on many levels, social and interactive. A primary capacity of the person, and one which facilitates both individual and social growth, is the capacity to experience another's reality as one's own while at the same time retaining a sense of one's unique identity.

What none of the secular theories really plumbs, although they may skirt around the edges of it, is the depth or the spiritual dimension of that network. Here the traditional Catholic doctrine comes in. Theologian Hans Urs von Balthasar puts it well:

> . . . the saints [have] grasped the principle which welds them together . . . unity as being-for-one-another . . . [which is] is a total reversal of human relationships and structures . . . the communion of saints interpenetrate each other and are woven seamlessly together.[45]

Von Balthasar speaks of this principle that the saints have grasped in a manner bounded by traditional Christian dogmatic perimeters. He sees the source of the "unity" of which this "being-for-one-another" consists, as the Holy Spirit. The Spirit communicates the very nature of the Godhead itself (which is being-for-one-another) to the whole body of Christ, the Church. He likewise sees the "total reversal of self-identity" that being-for-one-another implies as supernaturally imparted. Humans, in their "natural" state he conceives of as having "bright spiritual apexes of consciousness . . . distinct and opposed to each other." Certainly this latter view of the intrinsic psychic nature of humankind is challenged by research like that going on at the Stone Center. Might such an assumption be derived from a model of humanity that does not take women's self-consciousness into account? Despite this, and despite that ecclesiology that undergirds what he is saying, at root Von Balthasar's instinct and the organic metaphor he uses resonate harmoniously with what I am saying here. And he dips into the depth, or mystical, dimension of the metaphor most poetically.

"Being-for-one-another" is not a prescription for how we should "selflessly" act if we were but truly Christian but a more foundational description of our deepest identity. That we are first and foremost being-for-one-another or self-in-relation is an essential part of human self-knowledge. Our self is larger than we commonly perceive. It is unbounded, surpassing even the historical limits of our present relationships. Our self is bounded only by the boundless mystery of the divine life itself. At the same time, it should be noted that this does not mean that the commonly perceived self is obliterated by the larger reality, but that it is made vital and actualized only by understanding its unique self as an essential part of a dynamically interdependent whole.

Reading Saints' Lives

This leads us rather circuitously back to Saint Aloysius and his *Life*. If he and I are being-for-one-another, selves-in-relation in a manner that transcends historicity, then perhaps he is more than a model for me. For to model myself on him requires my pushing aside more cultural baggage than I'm sure it's worth. I could find more comfortable models closer at hand, others who had also heroically resisted the dehumanizing social mores of other centuries in the name of Christ. If he and I are truly in communion with each other in a sense that goes well beyond the notion that we share the name of Christian, then he and I participate in each other's lives in a radical way.

In a manner not dissimilar from the way family-systems analysts talk about patterns of interaction replicating themselves from generation to generation in families, so too that severe young Jesuit novice and I share a common history and patterning of consciousness that connects us. He is not simply my forebear in the sense that he precedes me in time, but that in the substructure of my being, his life and mine are interconnected. What he experienced at the deepest levels of his being, the choices he made, live in the deepest level of my being. They are part of my family history, part of the unconsciously encoded patterning that informs the actions I seemingly make as a discreet individual. Just as the forgotten habits of violence or nonviolence, of gender expectation, of achievement or failure, of unresolved pain or recurrent illness, continue to manifest themselves intergenerationally in families, so too Aloysius' tenacity in resisting the lascivious life into which he was born and his passionate embrace of the principles of Christian asceticism and prayer belong to me. They are in my bones, my blood, my family history.

This spiritual connection between the Italian prince turned novice and myself is, from the viewpoint of Christian theology, forged by the unifying action of the Holy Spirit which acts and moves in each Christian from the moment of baptism. Karl Rahner develops this idea in his reflections on sanctity by claiming that the saints are initiators of new, creative forms of the Christian life that are appropriate for their own days. The many interconnected forms of holy living spring from one inexhaustible source, the holiness of Christ, which continues to unfold itself in the history of the Church.[46] While I certainly do not wish to reject this general idea (especially in the dynamic way Rahner develops it), I would think that it might be extended well beyond the exclusive confines of Christian doctrinal formulation to speak to a fundamental spiritual interpenetration that all persons share to a greater or lesser degree of consciousness. Thus the lived perception of true human identity, of precisely this self-in-relation, this being-for-one-another, is the realm of the saints (from whatever tradition).[47] Keenly aware of the subtly interpenetrating lives that we live, they live authentically (as concretely defined by the religious sensibilities of their separate times and spaces) a knowing life of participation. The divine ground which we all share is the locus of their consciousness.

Whatever of love or heroism or religiously inspired audacity, whatever wide generosity, quickened compassion, or luminosity of vision that Aloysius had are not only mine for emulation, they are mine to plumb, by which to be strengthened and nourished. To put it more concretely and using a Christian framework, the fund of his most authentic prayer exists in a sacred "space" and "time" transcending both history and locale. It is the same space and time in which my most authentic prayer is born and uttered. It is the same space and time in which Aloysius' most authentic prayer was and *is* uttered. For we are part of one archingly transcendent human motion toward the divine. I can claim his hope, his desire, his faith as my own. We are in communion, and that communion is a dynamic, interactive one that explodes the boundaries of my little self beyond my historic moment, beyond the particular circumstances of my life, beyond even my imagining.

As I read the *Life of Aloysius Gonzaga* I am, as it were, regressing into the buried consciousness of my family history to discover there the sources, the directions, and the history of my most real self. I am discovering the dimension of human existence that unites us. The transcendent acts that he made there are continually etched on the substructure of my life and vitally affect me. His prayer is part of the history of my own. It is even more than that, it is my own. In communion with that rather odd, even off-putting young man from the sixteenth century, I am praying and struggling to actualize the deepest potential of my being. In communion with the saints, we all move to the consummation of the most radical hopes and the most treasured desires of the human family's heart. As strange as it may seem to her, that family — that communion — includes both my impatient pre-teen daughter and the "weird" Saint Aloysius. And that, I believe, is not a facile or sentimental truism but a religious insight of the most profound order.

NOTES

1. This piece is not intended to be an academic study of Aloysius but an exploration, combining recent scholarship and personal theological reflection, on the reading of a saint's life, in this case Saint Aloysius', in the shifting context of late-twentieth-century Catholic religious sensibilities.

2. Quoted in Father V. Cepari, S.J., *Saint Aloysius Gonzaga* (New York: Benziger Brothers, 1891), 256. Other classic biographies of the saint are C.C. Martindale, S.J., *The Vocation of Aloysius Gonzaga* (St. Louis, Mo.: B. Herder Book Co., 1927 and the same author's briefer treatment in *In God's Army*, Vol. III, *Christ's Cadets* (London: Burns, Oates and Washbourne, 1923).

3. Cepari, 271-326.

4. Carolyn Walker Bynum in her recent *Holy Feast, Holy Fast* (Berkeley, Calif.: Univ. of California Press, 1987) is at the forefront of this uncovering in the American academy.

5. For an approach of this type, see Donald Weinstein and Rudolf Bell, *Saints and Society: The Two Worlds of Western Christendom*, 1000-1700 (Chicago: University of Chicago Press, 1986).

6. Cf. William M. Thompson, *Fire and Light: The Saints and Theology* (New York/Mahwah, N.J.: Paulist Press, 1987).

7. As does Clifford Stevens in the introduction to this volume.

8. See Kate Simon, *A Renaissance Tapestry. The Gonzaga of Mantua* (New York: Harper and Row, 1988).

9. On a reappraisal of the body in Christian spirituality, see Margaret R. Miles, *Fullness of Life: Historical Foundations for a New Asceticism* (Westminster, John Knox, 1981).

10. Lawrence S. Cunningham, *The Meaning of Saints* (San Francisco: Harper and Row, 1980).

11. *The Life of Saint Martin, Bishop of Tours* by Sulpicius Severus in *The Western Fathers*, trans. and ed. F.R. Hoare (New York: Harper and Row, 1965, 10-44).

12. On a critique of the process, see Cunningham, 34-61.

13. Walter J. Burghardt, S.J., *Saints and Sanctity* (Englewood Cliffs, N.J.: Prentice Hall, 1965).

14. *Ibid.*, vii.

15. Shawn Madigan, *Models of Holiness Derived from the Saints*

of Universal Significance in the Roman Calendar (Ph.D. Dissertation 1984, Catholic University).

16. In the case of most popular contemporary saints, it is their devotion to the poor that is most notable. This may be expressed either apolitically, as is the case of Mother Teresa, or politically, as was the case with Oscar Romero. In any case, an acute awareness of the suffering of the disadvantaged and heroic action on their behalf, to the extent of taking on their lot or even dying as witness to their plight, seems often to single out persons for recognition as "saints" today.

At the same time there is still interest in the more traditional model of wonder-worker. Padre Pio, Italian stigmatic, is the object of intense devotion in certain segments of today's Catholic world.

For other recent authors doing some new naming, see Archbishop Rembert Weakland, "Story of a Saint of the 1990s" in *Origins*, Vol. 19, No. 33 (Jan. 18, 1990), 534-37; Mary Lou Kownacki, O.S.B., "One Day at A Time" in *Pax Christi*, Vol. 12, No. 2 (Summer 1987) for an article on Etty Hillesum, as patron saint of resistance; Tessa Bielecki, "Marks of Compassion" in *Pax Christi* (Vol. 14, No. 2 (Summer 1989), 4-6, on the contemporary exemplary qualities of saints, including human frailty, fidelity to the details of life, "bounce," and hilarity among others; James Breig, "Somebody Up There Likes Me. What U.S. Catholic Readers Believe About the Saints," *U.S. Catholic* (Nov. 1987), 6-15. It should also be noted that contemporary iconographer Robert Lentz has enjoyed popular success by creating icons of the revered, if unofficial, "saints" of our own times. His work is available through *Bridge Building Icons*, Burlington, Vermont.

17. Elizabeth Johnson, "Communion of Saints: Partners on the Way," *Church* (Summer 1989), 18.

18. Peter Brown, *The Cult of the Saints: Its Rise and Function in Late Christianity* (Chicago: University of Chicago Press, 1982).

19. For an interesting theological exploration of this very issue see Karl Rahner, "Prayer to the Saints" in *The Courage to Pray* (New York: Crossroad, 1981), 31-87. It has been pointed out to me that, despite the fact that most contemporary Christians seem ambivalent about the dead as companions, the deceased are felt to be a very present reality for those who are in solidarity with the struggles of the Church in Latin America. "*¡Presente!*" is the common acclamation

called forth when the names of the martyred are spoken in liturgical celebration.

20. For a sustained discussion of these changing Christian images of the Church, Christ, and time, see Madigan, *Models of Holiness*. She sees the difficulty in the current calendar as due to the fact that the Vatican II document that deals with the call to holiness and the Pilgrim Church, *The Constitution on the Church*, falls midway in the Council and reflects both the pre- and postconciliar divergent world views.

21. Selden P. Delany, in his *Married Saints* (New York: Longmans, Green and Co., 1935), 5-9, states the classic pre-Vatican II understanding of sanctity and its intrinsic relationship to the evangelical counsels of poverty, chastity and obedience with remarkable clarity:

> Is sanctity incompatible with marriage? . . . Most of the saints commemorated in the church's calendar have been bishops, priests or religious. Many of the canonized married saints were either martyrs or royal saints who married for reasons of state or who separated by mutual consent and became religious, or when the husband or wife died the other embraced the monastic life. It must be admitted that few married women, whose husbands outlived them, have been canonized. There have been many saintly widows, but a husband in the flesh seems to be an obstacle to sanctity. . . .
>
> To assert that men and women may become saints in the married state, if marriage is their vocation, is not to assert that there is no difference in merit — that is in the rewards they will receive in heaven — between those who follow the evangelical counsels of poverty, chastity and obedience, and those who live merely according to the commandments.

22. Johnson, "Communion of Saints," 19.

23. On the early inclusion of the phrase in credal formulas, consult Philip Schaff, *The Creeds of Christendom*, Vol. I, *The History of the Creed*, reprint of 1877 original (Grand Rapids, MI: Baker Book House, 1977) and Emilion Lamirande, O.M.I., *The Communion of Saints*, 15-24, Vol. 26 of the *Twentieth Century Encyclopedia of Catholicism*, ed. Henri Daniel-Rops (New York: Hawthorne Books, 1963).

24. For the Catholic presentation, see Paul Molinari, S.J., *Saints: Their Place in the Church* (New York: Sheed and Ward, 1965); Henri de Lubac, *Theological Fragments* (San Francisco: Ignatius Press, 1989), esp. 11-34 and 71-75; Hans Urs von Balthasar, *Elucidations* (London, SPCK, 57-63); and Karl Rahner, *Theological Investigations*, Vol. 3, *Theology of the Spiritual Life* (Baltimore, Helicon Press, 1961), 91-104.

25. For an especially clear presentation of this see Christoph Schonborn, "The 'Communion of Saints' as Three States of the Church," *Communio*, XV, No. 2 (Summer 1988), 169-81. This whole issue of the journal devotes itself to the communion of saints.

26. Molinari gives a complete treatment of this, presenting a pre-Vatican II synthesis. See also Lamirande, *op. cit.*

27. I make these observations mainly from interactions with my classes in Christian spirituality and pastoral ministry.

28. For an interesting discussion by a Protestant theologian on Christian worship and the saints, see James Wm. McClendon, Jr., *Biography as Theology: How Life Stories Can Remake Today's Theology* (Nashville, Abingdon Press, 1974). For a more systematic treatment of the doctrine from a Protestant perspective, see Wolfhart Pannenberg, *The Apostles' Creed in the Light of Today's Theology* (Philadelphia, Westminster Press, 1972), 144-159; Dietrich Bonhoeffer, *The Communion of Saints; A Domestic Inquiry Into the Sociology of the Church* (New York: Harper & Row). For a historical study of the apprehension of saints and martyrs at the time of the Reformation, especially in the Lutheran churches, see Robert Kolb, *For All the Saints: Changing Perceptions of Martyrdom and Sainthood in the Lutheran Reformation* (Macon, Ga.: Mercer Press, 1987).

29. David M. Tracy, *The Analogical Imagination: Christian Theology and the Culture of Pluralism* (New York: Crossroad, 1981).

30. Andrew M. Greeley and Mary Greeley Durkin, in *How to Save the Catholic Church* (New York: Viking, 1984), present a popularized interpretation of Tracy's distinction which is helpful.

31. The "universal call to holiness" highlighted in the Vatican II document *De Ecclesia, Lumen Gentium*, or *Constitution on the Church* (1964) has been heard and taken seriously by all segments of

the American Church. But the specifics of what that means and the concrete images and works of holiness are understood in different ways.

32. The journal *Communio: International Catholic Review* (Indiana: University of Notre Dame) is representative of this trend. The raison d'être for its establishment was to provide a journal dedicated to the spiritual and theological renewal initiated by Vatican II. The theological scope of the publication distinguishes it quite clearly from the post-Vatican II segment of the Church which I have referred to as "Protestantized."

33. For instance, J. P. Kirsch, *The Doctrine of the Communion of Saints in the Ancient Church. A Study in the History of Doctrine*, trans. John R. M'Kee (Edinburgh: Sands, 1910).

34. On the martyrs, see Bernard McGinn and John Meyendorff, ed., *Christian Spirituality*, Vol 1, *Origins to the Twelfth Century*, World Spirituality Series (New York: Crossroad, 1985).

35. On this see Kirsch, *Doctrine of the Communion of Saints*, Ch. 1.

36. For example, Dominican Noel Alexander (1639-1724) admits to there being five meanings of the phrase "communion of saints."

37. Jodi Bilenkoff, focusing a new feminist social-cultural lens on Teresa of Ávila, comes up with a very familiar pattern of Christian commitment to a set of values and relationships that subvert the dominant cultural ones. See her *The Ávila of Saint Teresa: Religious Reform in a Sixteenth-Century City* (Cornell University Press, 1989).

38. Catherine of Siena poetically explores the richness of the biblical vine-and-branch image when speaking of the communal spiritual reality of the Church.

> You then are my workers, you have come from me, the supreme eternal gardener, and I have engrafted you onto the vine by making myself one with you.
>
> Keep in mind that each of you has your own vineyard. But everyone is joined to your neighbors' vineyards without any dividing lines. They are so joined together, in fact, that you cannot do good or evil for yourself without doing the same for your neighbors.
>
> All of you together make up one common vineyard, the whole

Christian assembly, and you are all united in the vineyard of the
mystic body of holy Church from which you draw your life.
— Catherine of Siena, *The Dialogue*, trans. Suzanne
Noffke, O.P. (New York: Paulist Press, 1980), 62.

39. It should be noted that I speak primarily of white middle-class
literate notions of self that prevail in American institutions. Black
Americans, Native Americans, and other ethnic minorities do not
necessarily share these common notions.

40. On American individualism, see especially Robert Bellah et al.,
Habits of the Heart: Individualism and Commitment in American Life
(Berkeley: University of California Press, 1985).

41. The complexity and far-reaching implications of the feminist
research across the spectrum of the academy cannot be easily cited.
Some indication of the scope of the movement in Christian theology is
documented in Anne E. Carr, *Transforming Grace, Christian
Tradition and Women's Experience* (San Francisco: Harper & Row,
1988).

42. Stone Center Work is most accessible through its *Working
Papers* available by writing to Wellesley College, Stone Center for
Developmental Services and Studies, 106 Central Street, Wellesley,
MA 02181. One of the most noted of the psychologists working there
is Jean Baker Miller. Her groundbreaking *Toward A New Psychology
of Women* (Cambridge, Mass.: Harvard University Press, 1982) is an
early example of the approach which has grown considerably beyond
that book's confines in recent years.

43. The literature in this emerging field is enormous. A few of the
classics are Rosemary Radford Ruether's *Sexism and God Talk:
Toward A Feminist Theology* (Boston: Beacon Press, 1983); Elisabeth
Schussler Fiorenza, *Bread Not Stone: The Challenge of Feminist
Biblical Interpretation* (Boston: Beacon Press, 1984); Carr's
Transforming Grace provides a good overview of the movement.

44. For a brief overview of Catholic social teaching, see Peter J.
Henriot, Edward P. DeBerri, Michael J. Schultheis, *Catholic Social
Teaching: Our Best Kept Secret* (Maryknoll, N.Y.: Orbis Books,
1988).

45. Hans Urs von Balthasar, *Elucidations* (London: SPCK, 1975),
57-63.

46. Karl Rahner, *Theological Investigations*, Vol. III, *The Theology of the Spiritual Life* (Baltimore: Helicon Press, 1961), 91-104.

47. I have tried elsewhere to discover a way of describing this perceptual awareness which, I would suggest, is somehow found in the recognized saints of most traditions. See my "For All the Saints" in *Weaving*, Vol. III, No. 5 (Sept./Oct. 1988), 6-18.

V

On Understanding the Saints

Richard C. Hermes, S.J.

Introduction:

I t is sometimes asserted today that the saints must be rescued from the hagiographers of the past to be made relevant for men and women of our time. Beyond such assertions, however, remarkably little work is actually being done to bring the great saints of the past back to light. One may begin to suspect, then, that it is not just the hagiographers who seem so antiquated and fail to move us but the saints themselves.

Part of our problem in understanding and being moved by the saints is a now-ingrained and reflexive historicist mentality. A historicist mentality in approaching the saints consists in refusing to take seriously the accounts of the lives of the saints given by their contemporaries. More radically, it is the belief that the saints are decisively limited by their own historical horizon and are thus without meaning for our age or any other but their own. Thus understood, no one saint can teach the whole Church. Each saint is relevant to his contemporaries alone. The historicist reduces the communion of saints to a mere succession of saints.

The essential note of sanctity, the imitation of Christ, is timeless. Therefore, the necessary condition for understanding the sanctity of any saint is an understanding of the Gospel. However, the note of sanctity is played in an infinite variety of keys corresponding severally to each saint's existential situation. Consequently, the sufficient condition is surely a true understanding of each saint's personal life and historical age. This, I maintain, cannot be done unless we first approach a given saint and his age as though each has something to teach us. By doing so we avoid the mistake of assuming our understanding of the saints to be superior to their self-understanding and the understanding of them by their contemporaries.

The guiding assumption of this essay is that the first, and indeed, the classical biographer and contemporary of Saint Aloysius Gonzaga, Virgilio Cepari, understood him correctly and preserved the essential character of his sanctity in that first *Life*. It seems to me that this assumption has the most practical kind of necessity. For if Cepari cannot be trusted to have got it right, then no one following Cepari, in light of their complete dependence on him, can be reliably trusted. Least of all can we today, given our remove from the sixteenth century and our alienation from its spiritual milieu and outlook, be expected to understand Aloysius without Cepari's Life. My aim, then, is simple: to communicate the results of one particular reading of Cepari's *Life of Saint Aloysius Gonzaga*, one that concentrates as much as possible on Cepari's understanding of the sanctity of Aloysius.[1]

Background and Character of Aloysius Gonzaga

On the face of it, the character of Gonzaga is not likely to attract many of our contemporaries. The kind of hidden perfection he sought, it must be admitted, is out of fashion in our egalitarian age; likewise, his unyielding fidelity to the will of God strikes the modern, easy-going mentality as in bad taste. Conditioned as we are by the secular, Aloysius can appear otherworldly. There is no better antidote to such appraisals of Gonzaga than Cepari's *Life*.

From the beginning, Cepari reveals Aloysius as a passionate, intelligent young man who, though born and reared in the court life of the Renaissance, rejected all its enticements and embraced the *via crucis* with a brutal realism, completely devoid of sentimentality. Cepari begins with the family background of Aloysius, situating him as the heir to the marquisate of Don Ferrante Gonzaga, a prince of the Holy Roman Empire. On his mother's side, Aloysius was the second cousin to the Cardinal Archbishop of Turin. In addition, his mother was a confidential maid of honor to Isabel de Valois, the Queen of Philip II and daughter of Henry II of France. Given this lineage and these connections, we are not surprised later to find Aloysius serving as a page to James the Prince at the court of Philip II, or playing as a child with one of the Medicis, Marie, the future Queen of France.

If Aloysius seems overly-precocious in some of the childhood events related by Cepari, it is important to recall the rarified atmosphere of court life. As the son of a prince, Aloysius was almost constantly accompanied by attendants of his own; he was dressed daily and cared for in every way; he spent significant periods of his youth in the company of adults assigned to him as private tutors and body servants; and he was given an exceptional education.

Aloysius showed intellectual promise at a very young age. He began to study Latin and Italian at the age of nine. Cepari reports that his favorite classical authors were Plutarch, Seneca, and Valerius Maximus. While at the Spanish court, he learned logic, mathematics, and philosophy. According to Cepari, he combined his academic acumen with uncommonly good sense and a maturity beyond his years. Even before the age of sixteen, it was apparently not unusual for the Marquis to entrust Aloysius with family business.

Cepari depicts Aloysius as a naturally vigorous and attractive person, adept in both physical and mental pursuits. The rigor of his spiritual life, the solitude he constantly sought, his "purity of mind" as Cepari puts it, "cannot be attributed to him because of any natural coldness and sluggishness, for he was full of life and spirit, activity and alertness, as all knew who were acquainted with him."[3] Likewise, Cepari makes plain, his persistent sickliness was the result of excessive self-mortification rather than a weak body. Regarding the toll these practices had taken on the health of Aloysius by his eleventh year, Cepari observes, "The result was that, though up to that time he had been rather stout and healthy-looking, he became thin and withered."[4]

The Union of Saint Aloysius with Christ Crucified

In popular iconography, Saint Aloysius is often pictured holding a large crucifix. This is an apt image. For the overriding theme of his life, the center and unity of his spirituality, the motivating source of his harsh and (to us) excessive physical penances, was his desire to unite himself spiritually and physically with the passion and death of

Christ. If anything stands out in Cepari's *Life* it is an appreciation of this wellspring of Gonzaga's spirituality.

Contrary to our contemporary practice of replacing the spiritual act of fasting with the vain one of dieting, an eleven-year-old Aloysius began with a rigorous medical diet (prescribed to overcome a bout of strangury), and eventually embraced abstinence, "as he told Father Jerome Piatti . . . no longer for the sake of his health . . . but out of devotion."[5] Gradually, Aloysius added to his fixed fasts and abstinences great corporal disciplines: self-inflicted scourgings, the wearing of hairshirts, and long hours of prayer on his knees. Cepari describes these penances vividly:

> "He disciplined himself to blood, at least three times a week. And during the last years he spent in the world, he scourged himself every day, and finally even three times each day and this even to blood. As at first he had not got a discipline, he beat himself sometimes with dogs' leashes, which he chanced to have, or with pieces of rope, and — so some have said — with an iron chain. Oftentimes those who waited on him found him on his knees in his room taking the discipline; and when they made his bed, they discovered hidden under the bolster the scourges of cord which he used. Several times his sheets were shown to his mother, all stained with blood."[6]

Although his fasts and disciplines were greatly curbed by his religious superiors once he entered the novitiate, Aloysius never gave them up altogether. As one would expect, this had serious consequences for his health. He ruined his stomach early on, so that even had he been so inclined he would have been unable to take in much food. Because of the intensity of his prayer late at night (often prostrate on the cold stone floor) and the consequent lack of sleep, Aloysius was wracked by excruciating headaches which tortured him most of his life. After he died, great callouses were found on his knees formed by the years of frequent kneeling without cushions. Cepari neither hesitates to recount these incidents nor withholds his own judgment of them. He writes:

"There is no doubt that in his fervor he went beyond all bounds and reason; but he thought he was right in doing so, and as he had no one to guide him, he let his fervor be his director."[7]

For Cepari, Aloysius' youthful mortifications, though excessive, are understandable and even laudable insofar as they were the result of his single-minded pursuit of God's will. It was that same single-minded obedience which led him to moderate these practices as a Jesuit. Corporal punishment was never a self-centered end in itself for Aloysius. Cepari understands this well. He knows that Aloysius embraced a life of penance and self-denial ". . . out of a desire to suffer and be like in somewhat to Christ our Lord in his crowning with thorns. . . ."[8]

This total dedication to our Lord, this complete renunciation of himself to be at God's disposal, this burning desire of Saint Aloysius to share in the passion of Christ becomes most clear in Cepari's moving account of his death.

Aloysius returned to Rome for the final time in May of 1590 to resume his study of theology. He had just resolved the dispute between his brother Rodolph and William the Duke of Mantua.[9] From this point on, Cepari's *Life* takes on a sense of inevitability leading inexorably to the only event that could unite Aloysius perfectly with Christ — a holy death. It was around this time that Aloysius related to Bellarmine what Cepari calls an "interior illumination" of his approaching death.

In Cepari's description of the ten weeks Aloysius lay on his deathbed, two things are striking: the real joy of Aloysius at his imminent death, and the overwhelming sadness of his Jesuit brethren at losing him. Cepari recounts one incident which captures the mood of all concerned:

"Shortly after, one of his fellow-scholastics came into his room and [Aloysius] said merrily to him: 'Father, *laetantes imus, laetantes imus* — we are going and gladly.' And these words, which he said so joyfully, made the rest sigh and weep."[10]

On another occasion, after Aloysius spoke matter-of-factly to the Provincial of going to heaven, the Provincial was heard to say, "Just hear him! He talks of going to heaven as we would talk of going to Frascati."[11]

Cepari makes it plain that Aloysius, who took ill serving the sick and whose great desire was always to serve in the missions, did not anticipate death as an escape from this life so much as a perfect participation in the one fully human life — that of Christ, who became man even to the point of death. On the night of Aloysius' death, Cepari himself was attending the bedside. He noticed Aloysius remove his headcap. Cepari silently replaced it. When Aloysius removed it again, Cepari admonished him gently to protect his head from the air. Aloysius said, "Christ had nothing on his head when he died."[12] Cepari writes of his own thoughts, "His words touched me and filled me with devotion and compunction, for I then perceived that even at that moment his whole thought was to imitate Christ on the cross."[13]

Several hours later, at the moment of death, Aloysius spoke once more and asked to be shifted in bed a little, as he had not been moved for three days. The two Fathers who were present, fearful of hastening his death by any movement, reminded him of the sufferings of Christ at His death. They lit a candle, blessed Aloysius with it, and offered it to him. Cepari concludes the story:

> "Aloysius grasped it, in sign of perseverance in the holy faith, and
> with it in his hand, a short time afterwards he made an effort to
> invoke the most holy name of Jesus. He, at last, just moved his lips,
> and between 10 and 11, with perfect peace, he gave up his soul to
> His Creator."[14]

Saint Aloysius and the Spiritual Authorities

Cepari's *Life*, based largely on interviews with those who knew Aloysius, features prominently the testimony of several holy and authoritative contemporaries of the young saint. It is instructive to look with Cepari at the great affection and esteem for Aloysius expressed by four of these "holy authorities" — two saints and cardinals, Robert Bellarmine and Charles Borromeo, and two Jesuit spiritual writers, Jerome Piatti and Achille Gagliardi.

Robert Bellarmine

The greatest Jesuit theologian of the time, Cardinal Robert Bellarmine, was Gonzaga's last confessor and probably his most intimate friend. He was certainly Gonzaga's greatest admirer and promoter. After the friendship between Ignatius and Francis Xavier, that of Bellarmine and Gonzaga must rank as the most fruitful and important friendship for the development and propagation of Jesuit spirituality.

In Cepari's *Life*, Bellarmine appears as the crucial and authoritative source for the spiritual life of Saint Aloysius. As his confessor and spiritual father for most of the final three years of Gonzaga's life, Bellarmine had an important role in the formation of Aloysius as a Jesuit. In turn, Aloysius served as Bellarmine's model for sanctity and later as his advocate in heaven. After the death of Aloysius, Bellarmine wrote to Cepari, ". . . I have never scrupled to recommend myself to his prayers, and I have great confidence in them."[15] Bellarmine's devotion to Aloysius was so great that the cult of Saint Aloysius within the Society may be said to have been begun and given its definitive form by Bellarmine.[16]

Time and again Aloysius relied on Bellarmine, his confessor and spiritual father, to shed light on his own spiritual struggles. However, Bellarmine's own testimony makes it plain that he considered *himself* the spiritual disciple of the much younger Gonzaga. To illustrate this, Cepari relates the following story:

> "[W]hile Cardinal Bellarmine was giving the Spiritual Exercises to some Scholastics of the Society in the Roman College, when suggesting admirable hints as to how to make their meditations, he used to say: 'I learned that from our Aloysius.' "[17]

What emerges from the pages of Cepari is a relationship of familiarity and trust between Cardinal Bellarmine and Aloysius Gonzaga. Bellarmine is there at the end to offer up the last prayers for the dying Aloysius.

> "Besides the two Fathers, just named, there stayed with him Father

Bellarmine and Father Vitelleschi. Father Robert said to S. Aloysius, that when he thought it was time, he should give him notice to say the recommendation of a departing soul, and the Saint replied that he would do so. Shortly after he said: 'Now, Father, it is time,' and the Father knelt down with the others and went through the prayers."[18]

Charles Borromeo

Charles Borromeo, a cardinal of the Church and bishop of Milan, was a towering figure of the Catholic Reformation. He oversaw the catechism, missal, and breviary called for by the Council of Trent. He developed the system of seminaries for the education of the clergy. In many ways, Borromeo was the great apostle and missionary of the Council and of Church reform.

One of Cepari's most memorable vignettes, and one significant for establishing the early sanctity of Aloysius, is the encounter between the great ecclesiastic Borromeo and the twelve-year-old Gonzaga in the summer of 1580. Borromeo was in Castiglione on a papal-appointed visitation of the bishoprics of his province. Cepari relates that Aloysius, motivated by the holy reputation of the Cardinal, visited Borromeo at the local parish church.

The scene that unfolds is not that the familiar one of an important, busy man perfunctorily receiving a visit from the fawning son of a local noble. Instead, Cepari notes that Borromeo took genuine delight at Gonzaga's visit and "made him remain so long with him in his room to talk on heavenly things, that those waiting outside were quite annoyed."[19] One can only guess at the impact of Gonzaga's youthful but explosive form of sanctity on Borromeo. For by that time Aloysius was astonishingly well-advanced in the spiritual life — he had received the gift of tears, he had privately vowed himself to a life of chastity, he had resolved to become a priest, and for years he had been engaged in a rigorous regime of fasting.

Commenting on the benefits to Aloysius, Cepari says he "was delighted to have found someone to whom he could with confidence open his heart and ask for a solution of the doubts which he met with in the spiritual life."[20] Borromeo, upon learning that Gonzaga was not a communicant, not only urged him to receive the Eucharist but spiritually prepared him for it and administered his First Communion.

The meeting of these two saints, contemporaries, but so opposite temperamentally, and with such different missions in the Church, seems providential. The full depth of their mutual spiritual influence, like so much of God's inner action, must remain hidden. What is noteworthy for our understanding of Aloysius today, when the very possibility of holiness among the young is cynically dismissed, is the obviously great impression Gonzaga's youthful holiness made on Borromeo, a holy man of great stature, both as scholar and diplomat.

Jerome Piatti

There are only two written sources for the life of Aloysius which are older than Cepari's first complete *Life*. One is the manuscript of notes taken by Father Jerome Piatti during the saint's lifetime.[21] These notes were handed over to Cepari, formed the basis for his first *Life*, and were fully incorporated into it.

Piatti was born to a wealthy Milanese family in 1545, entered the Society in 1568, and died at the age of forty-four in 1591, two months after Saint Aloysius. He was rector of the professed college of the Gesù in Rome, where he first met Aloysius. Later, he served as the secretary of the French and German Jesuit assistancies. In addition to his administrative work, he was a well-known member of that generation of spiritual writers which flourished under Claudius Aquaviva's generalate.[22]

Given Piatti's influence, both administratively and spiritually, in the years of expansion and institutionalization of the Jesuit Order, Cepari rightly recognizes him as well-situated to appreciate the impact of Gonzaga's entrance into the Order. This appraisal is stated clearly in a letter Piatti wrote to the future Jesuit General, Mutius Vitelleschi, then a scholastic studying at Naples. In the letter, written just a few days after Gonzaga's entrance, Piatti recounts with palpable excitement the considerable stir caused in the Order by Gonzaga's arrival.

"I cannot make a better reply . . . than by giving you an account of a distinguished novice who entered S. Andrea five days ago . . . a youth, by name Aloysius Gonzaga . . . His abilities are such that his rank is his least distinction; for although he is not yet eighteen years old, and has spent so much time in Court, he is already well grounded in both logic and natural science. . . . But all this is nothing compared to his virtue and sanctity. . . . You must know, then, that of gifts of nature and grace, the only one that is wanting to Aloysius is his health; for he is so delicate that only to look on him fills one with fear. . . . So pray for him and be sure that, if God gives him life and health, you will see him do great things for the service of God and the Society."[23]

Later during Gonzaga's novitiate, when the novices were sent to the Professed House in Rome, Piatti, as rector of the house, had charge of Gonzaga and served as his confessor. It was Piatti who made the memorably solemn declaration after visiting Aloysius on his deathbed, "I tell you Aloysius is a saint, most certainly a saint, and so great a saint that he could be canonized in his lifetime."[24]

Achille Gagliardi

Gagliardi was born in 1537 and entered the Society of Jesus with his two brothers in 1559. He went through the Jesuit course of studies with Robert Bellarmine and later taught philosophy and theology at the Roman College. Gagliardi was one of the Society's early authorities on the *Spiritual Exercises*. He was also considered an expert on what was known as mystical theology.

Gagliardi's first acquaintance with Aloysius was as the last of a string of interrogators charged by Gonzaga's father to test the youth's vocation. Gagliardi had two points which recommended him to Don Ferrante as a choice examiner — his reputation for learning and holiness and his membership in the Society. In fact, by Gonzaga's own account, Gagliardi was the most difficult and persuasive objector. Cepari reports that for a whole hour Gagliardi offered objections as though they were his own. The answers he received were so convincing that Father Gagliardi finally exclaimed, "Signor Aloysius, you are right. It certainly is as you have said. There is no doubt about it. You have both edified and satisfied me."[25]

Cepari reports that four years later, during Gonzaga's stay in the Jesuit house in Milan, Gagliardi frequently sought Aloysius out for spiritual conversation. Apparently, Aloysius' reputation for having "an extraordinary gift of prayer free from distractions of any sort"[26] stirred Gagliardi's "mystical" interests. Cepari writes, "In [Gagliardi's] judgment the Saint had already reached to a height in prayer to which very few even of the most experienced and steadfast in religious life are given the grace to attain."[27] Cepari goes on to report that Gagliardi considered Aloysius' gift of divine union so great that he was compelled for love of God "to descend from the heights of contemplation to minister"[28] for the salvation of all men. "Hence," Cepari writes, "from that time forth [Gagliardi] went about proclaiming everywhere this great gift of S. Aloysius, and in three of his writings he has deposed to the same on oath."[29]

Aloysius Gonzaga and the Spirituality of Ignatius

The French Jesuit Father Joseph de Guibert, identified the peculiar and distinctive trait of Ignatian spirituality as "a union of surging enthusiasm and of reason."[30] Put another way, this union of enthusiasm and reason is the fusion of self-abandonment to the will of God in prayer with the rational, relentlessly practical consideration (discernment) of the best way to work God's will in the world. In short, it is the life of the contemplative in action. Cepari's *Life* reveals Saint Aloysius as thoroughly Ignatian in this fundamental way.

For Cepari, the nature of Gonzaga's enthusiastic union with God seems to be defined by the presence of two great gifts, perfect chastity and prayer. In Florence, at the age of nine, "while praying in the Church of the Annunziata before the picture placed there in her honor, he made a vow to God of perpetual chastity."[31] This vow, which Aloysius' confessors testify he kept perfectly, is judged by Cepari as "an extraordinary grace from God, and a remarkable favor of the most blessed Virgin."[32] Three years later, at Castiglione, Aloysius was given the gift of a near-constant capacity and desire for contemplation. He began to pray so constantly and so intensely that his servants, who peeked in his room through chinks in the door, "were astonished to see that for whole hours he would lie prostrate before a crucifix with his arms extended . . . as he gazed on the image of his Lord, all the while crying so bitterly that his sobs and sighs could be heard outside."[33] These gifts of chastity and prayer, emphasized by Cepari, seem in Aloysius very much like De Guibert's "surging enthusiasm."

Shortly after receiving the gift of prayer, Aloysius came upon a little work by the Jesuit theologian Peter Canisius, which helped him order his intense meditations.[34] According to Cepari, Aloysius not only gained from this work the courage to meditate, "but he was also taught what method to follow and at what time to make his meditation."[35] From the first, then, his enthusiastic life of contemplation was given order and method and direction under Jesuit influences.

This fusion of enthusiastic love and rational judgment never left Aloysius. The enthusiasm can be seen in his fiery determination, in spite of great opposition from his father, to enter religious life. The rational and realistic power of judgment shines through in his actual decision to enter the Society of Jesus. After considering a number of religious institutes and monastic orders, and rejecting them each in turn, he chose the Jesuits, according to Cepari, for four motives.

"The first was because religious observance was there in its first vigor and was preserved in all the purity of the Institute . . . the second was because the Society makes a special vow not to seek after any ecclesiastical dignities, nor to accept one when offered, unless by order of the Pope . . . the third was that he saw the Society had so many ways, by schools and sodalities, to aid in the bringing up of youth in the fear of God and the virtue of purity . . . the fourth reason was that the Society expressly embraced the work of the conversion of heretics . . . and the evangelization of the heathen in India, in Japan, and in the new world."[36]

This was the "Jesuit" core from which the whole spiritual life of Gonzaga, with its particular thrust, springs: a passionate, zealous pursuit of union with God in prayer directed by reason toward the loving service of others.

Nothing better indicates the Jesuit or Ignatian character of Gonzaga's spiritual life than the act of renunciation of the marquisate and his embrace of the evangelical counsels under the Jesuit constitutions. In the *Spiritual Exercises of Saint Ignatius*, the retreatant is called upon in the "Kingdom Meditation" to compare successively

the ready obedience and service owed by subjects to their temporal
king, with the obedience and service owed to "Christ our Lord, the
Eternal King, before whom is assembled the whole world."[37] Just as
the loyal subject must obey the call of his temporal king, the follower
of Christ must heed these words addressed to him by Christ,
"[W]hoever wishes to join me in this enterprise must be willing to
labor with me, that by following me in suffering, he may follow me in
glory."[38]

The "Kingdom Meditation" came to life in Aloysius Gonzaga.
He was confronted by earthly service and loyal obedience to his own
father's wishes from the very beginning. Aloysius never flouted his
father's authority. In fact, his last decisive appeal to the Marquis for
permission consisted in a radical act of obedience. He said, "Father, I
place myself entirely in your hands, do with me what you please. But
I declare to you that I have been called to the Society of Jesus by
God, and by your opposition to this vocation you are resisting the
will of God."[39]

Aloysius knew about court life and temporal service from the
inside. He knew what it was like to be both subject and master.
What's more, as he grew in knowledge and love of Christ, and saw
the totality of the demands made by obedience to Christ's kingship,
the "Kingdom Meditation" gave way to the "Meditation on the Two
Standards."[40] For Aloysius understood that once one has heeded the
call of Christ the King, any other allure, any other fundamental
attachment, falls under the banner of Satan. Aloysius sent one
message to his father the day he entered the novitiate, a quote from
Psalm 44: *Obliviscere populum tuum, et domum patris tui.*"[41] This
was the desire of Aloysius: to forget, to count as loss, all that would
distract from his service to Christ. For the follower of Christ, for
the one who embraces Christ's standard as Aloysius did, there is
only the life of "poverty as opposed to riches . . . insults or
contempt as opposed to the honor of this world . . . humility as
opposed to pride."[42]

This is the drama of the vocation and spirituality of Saint Aloysius
Gonzaga. Blessed with enormous intellectual abilities, a resolute but
gentle nature, and all the material advantages of the Renaissance court
life, Aloysius would have succeeded marvelously at that court life, a

master at its intrigues and affairs. But it would have meant compromising his union with God and abandoning his mission in the Church. When all is said and done, that would have been a serious betrayal of the Jesuit "manner of proceeding,"[43], which (when authentically followed) always leads one to communion with the triune God at the service of the Church.

Conclusion

Above all else, Cepari's *Life* is concerned with the relationship of Saint Aloysius with God. It is concerned with the spirituality of Saint Aloysius. Cepari, himself a son of Ignatius and long-schooled in the prayer of the *Spiritual Exercises*, finds a soul-mate of the deepest kind in Aloysius. In fact, Cepari finds in Aloysius Gonzaga a near-icon, an almost perfect representation of the Ignatian spirituality.

The chief theme, then, of Cepari's account may be said to be the way in which God led Gonzaga, beginning at an early age (long before he entered the Society of Jesus), along the Ignatian path to a mystical union with God, to a love for the divine rooted in a love for Jesus Christ, which necessarily impels one toward the loving service of others. In classic Ignatian fashion, Aloysius is a model for both mystics and missionaries. He is proof that the Jesuit ideal, *in actione contemplativus*, is attainable. For Cepari's generation, Aloysius appears dramatically, suddenly, as a gift from God to the Order, a living reminder and authentic renewal of those first spiritual experiences of Saint Ignatius himself which gave life and birth to the Society of Jesus.

NOTES

1. I have consulted two versions of Cepari's *Vita*: *The Life of Blessed Aloysius Gonzaga* (Paris, 1627), Vol. 201 of *English Recusant Literature*, ed. D.M. Rogers (Berkeley, Calif.: The Scolar Press, 1974) and *Life of Saint Aloysius Gonzaga* trans. Frederick Schroeder, S.J., ed. Francis Goldie, S.J. (New York: Benziger Brothers, 1891). Each has its own merits. The Recusant version is the more pristine publication. It is Cepari without a modern editor. Schroeder-Goldie is

more readable and includes some valuable notes but has tinkered slightly with Cepari's *editio princeps.*

2. For a lively treatment of the Gonzaga family and the Renaissance court, see Kate Simon, *A Renaissance Tapestry: The Gonzaga of Mantua* (New York: Harper and Row, 1988). See especially Chapter 13 for mention of Saint Aloysius.

3. Cepari, p. 18. All quotations from Cepari's *Life* are taken from the Schroeder-Goldie translation unless otherwise noted. The English of this edition, while somewhat dated, is still far easier-going than the Elizabethan translation of the Recusant series.

4. Ibid., p. 23.

5. Ibid., p. 22.

6. Ibid., p. 37.

7. Ibid., p. 82.

8. Ibid., p. 40.

9. Cepari gives a full account of this complex affair, which involved Aloysius in some delicate familial and diplomatic matters, in Part Two of the *Life*. Naturally, the journey was undertaken with the full permission of Aloysius' Jesuit superiors.

10. Cepari, p. 232.

11. Frascati was a place outside Rome used by the Jesuits for recreation and vacation.

12. Cepari, p. 237. In the Recusant Literature edition, Cepari quotes the Latin of this, *"Christus moriens capite operto non fuit,"* p. 397.

13. Ibid., pp. 237-238.

14. Ibid., p. 239.

15. Ibid., p. 256.

16. Especially important for the Society's traditional understanding of Aloysius is Bellarmine's sermon on Aloysius delivered on June 20, 1608. This can be found in its Latin original in the *Acta Sanctorum*, Junii, t. IV. as cited by Father James Broderick, *Blessed Robert Bellarmine* (Wilmette, Ill.: P.J. Kenedy and Sons, 1924), Vol. I, pp. 310-311.

17. Cepari, p. 133.

18. Ibid., p. 238.

19. Ibid., pp. 27-28.

20. Ibid., p. 28.

21. The other source is the vast amount of material collected by Father Giovanni Antonio Valtrino, one of the Society's early chroniclers, to whom Cepari had handed over his earliest notes. According to Father C.C. Martindale, in the introduction to his *The Vocation of Aloysius Gonzaga* (New York: Sheed and Ward, 1945), all the material from the two earlier sources was incorporated into Cepari's complete *Life*.

22. Aquaviva, the fifth General of the Society of Jesus, governed 1581-1615.

23. Cepari, pp. 120-124. That Piatti's insights were not idiosyncratic is confirmed by the existence of a widespread belief in the Society that Aloysius had been sent to the Order by God to become, one day, the General. In fact, he was sometimes referred to by the diminutive *Il Generalino*. See p. XI in Father Schroeder's Preface to Goldie's edition of the Life.

24. Ibid., p. 233.

25. Ibid., p. 77.

26. Ibid., pp. 208-209.

27. Ibid., p. 209.

28. Ibid., p. 210.

29. Ibid.

30. Joseph De Guibert, S.J., *The Jesuits: Their Spiritual Doctrine and Practice* (Rome: Institutum Historicum Societatis Iesu, 1953), trans. William J. Young, S.J., ed. George E. Ganss, S.J. (The Institute of Jesuit Sources, St. Louis, 1986), p. 175.

31. Cepari, p. 17.

32. Ibid., p. 18.

33. Ibid., p. 26.

34. This is almost certainly Canisius' little Catholic Catechism, sometimes called "*Catechismus parvus Catholicorum*." According to Goldie this enormously popular work went through more than fifty editions after it was first published in 1557.

35. Cepari, p. 26.

36. Ibid., pp. 52-53.

37. *The Spiritual Exercises of Saint Ignatius*, ed. Luis J. Puhl, S.J. (Loyola University Press, Chicago, 1951), no. 95.

38. Ibid.

39. Cepari, p. 86.

40. *The Spiritual Exercises*, nos. 136-148.

41. "Forget your people and your father's house." The Latin is from Cepari's *Life*, Recusant edition, p. 169.

42. *The Spiritual Exercises*, no. 146.

43. The time-honored phrase, *el modo de proceder*, of Saint Ignatius, popularized by Father Jerome Nadal. Nadal, a trusted companion of Saint Ignatius and the official interpreter of the Jesuit constitutions, composed in Spanish an unpublished work entitled *Dialogues*, in which he describes "the Society's manner of proceeding" in concise language. One passage in particular is worth citing for the light it sheds on the self-understanding of Jesuits by the time Cepari entered. Nadal writes, "They explain their vocation as a kind of light in Christ which seizes, motivates, and guides them; this begets a forward thrust and power of action by which, under the obedience of the hierarchical Roman Church, they struggle for the salvation and perfection of souls" (MHSI *Nadal,* V., p. 723).

VI

Aloysius Gonzaga's Exhortation to Young Nobles at the Jesuit College in Siena, May 1590

Joseph N. Tylenda, S.J.

With the coming of spring, and with the roads again suitable for travel, Aloysius set out from Milan, in early May 1590, with a small group of fellow Jesuits on their way to Rome. The domestic problems that had taken Aloysius from Rome to his native Castiglione were happily solved; his brother Rodolfo, Marquis of Castiglione, was reconciled to the Duke of Mantua and was acknowledged lord of Solferino as well.[1] It was time for Aloysius to return to his theological studies at the Roman College.

After an intermediate stop at Florence, the group traveled the thirty-three miles to Siena and lodged at the Jesuit college next to the church of San Vigilio, only a short walk from the city's main square. The Jesuits had opened a school in the city in May 1556. Nor was Aloysius unknown to that community; he had stopped there in mid-September 1589, on his way to Castiglione, and was remembered for having refused to yield to the custom, then common in Jesuit houses, of having a member of the host community wash the feet of the newly arrived guest. The refusal was both the expression of Aloysius' humility as well as the result of his embarrassment over the fuss that the Siena Jesuits were making over him. They seemed to have forgotten that he had abdicated the marquisate four and a half years previously.

The sojourn in Siena was brief, probably no more than two or three days. There was one item on his agenda, however, that Aloysius was most eager to accomplish, namely, to attend Mass and receive Communion in the room of Saint Catherine of Siena. One morning, he walked across the city with Father Pietro Alagona, who had joined the Rome-bound group in Florence; he served Alagona's Mass in the Benincasa home and received Holy Communion, as he had desired.

The origin of Aloysius' devotion to Saint Catherine remains unknown; perhaps it was his appreciation of her courage and resoluteness in convincing Pope Gregory XI that his place was in Rome and not in Avignon. Aloysius was familiar with Saint Catherine's letters,[2] and her tomb in the Roman church of Santa Maria sopra Minerva was but a stone's throw from his residence at the Roman College. The relics of Saint Catherine, who died in Rome in 1380, are now under the main altar, having been placed there in 1855, but in Aloysius' time they were in the Capranica chapel, right of the apse.

Taking advantage of Aloysius' presence at the college, some of the Jesuits in the community asked him to address the student members of Our Lady's Sodality. His humility, however, led him to decline the invitation — he would have to address the sons of Siena's nobility. But when the rector added his voice to that of the others, Aloysius interpreted the request as a command and immediately set about preparing what he would say. Father Cepari, Aloysius' principal biographer, informs us that he went to the chapel, gathered his thoughts together before the Blessed Sacrament, then went to his room. Recalling his past reading in the Fathers of the Church, he hastily put his thoughts on paper. What Aloysius wrote on that occasion follows these introductory remarks.

How many Jesuits of the Siena community attended Aloysius' talk is uncertain, but contemporary accounts indicate that the discourse was given with a certain vivacity and conviction. The students and faculty were impressed, not merely because of the content and manner of presentation, but notably by the young Jesuit's simplicity, sincerity, and evident holiness. When one of the community asked him for his notes so that he could copy them, Aloysius answered that he had somehow misplaced them. After his departure from Siena, Father Philip Ricci, who was at that time fully engaged in preaching, unexpectedly found them in a volume of Saint Bernard's works, which Aloysius had undoubtedly used in giving his discourse. Father Ricci, who had most probably attended the discourse, recognized the sheet of paper as the outline that Aloysius had used and immediately snatched it up. He then distributed copies to those requesting them.

In 1603, when Father Ricci was making his deposition during the canonical process held in Turin, prior to Aloysius' beatification, he said that he had kept the outline "with the greatest of care in his pulpit, being convinced that this little sheet of paper, covered with so virtuous a young man's writing, would some day be numbered among the most precious of objects and considered one of the most powerful cures for body and soul."[3] This autograph is today preserved in Collegio "Cesare Arici" in Brescia.[4]

Though Aloysius only wrote out an outline of his discourse, it is, nevertheless, a somewhat detailed outline. The few lacunae in the text indicate the places where Aloysius read from Saint Bernard — the text had been found in a volume of Bernard's works — or where he continued a citation from Saint Augustine or Saint Gregory from memory, together with his extempore comments. Since these texts are now supplied in the notes, it is not impossible for us to imagine how Aloysius developed his thoughts.

Aloysius gave no title to his discourse, but in essence it is an appeal to the students to use their talents for God. Thus he chose to quote James 1:22, informing the young nobles that it was not enough for them to be mere hearers of God's Word, but that they should be doers as well.

The discourse has two parts. In the first, Aloysius speaks of the three ways by which God speaks to the individual soul: (1) by secret inspirations, which are to nourish us internally; (2) by Scripture, to which we are to conform our lives; (3) by benefits, which we ought to return to God. Aloysius takes his arguments principally from Saint Bernard, who was one of his favorite authors.[5] So enamored was he of the abbot of Clairvaux, Cepari tells us, that since novitiate days Aloysius daily read a passage from his writings and later, when on his deathbed, he had Saint Augustine's *Soliloquies* and Saint Bernard's *Sermons on the Canticle of Canticles* read to him.[6] Since Aloysius' audience was the members of the Sodality, the school's better students, he was aware that he was speaking to youths who were talented and from whom great things could be expected. He, thus, reminds them that their talents are God-given and urges them to return them to God, that is, use them for God.

In the second part Aloysius tells his audience why they ought to fulfill what God tells them: (1) because it is God who speaks, a sufficient reason in itself, and (2) because God promises heaven. Conscious that the young men before him were of the Sienese nobility, and that the Grand Duke of Tuscany was soon to visit the school, Aloysius takes these facts into consideration and in this portion of his discourse adroitly adapts the Kingdom meditation from Ignatius of Loyola's *Spiritual Exercises* to the present circumstances. The answer to his question, "Who of us will be satisfied with hearing this invitation and not accept it, agree to this offer and not carry it out?" is inescapable. If anyone were to refuse to follow Christ, it could only be because he did not understand God's Word and because he was ignorant of the promises that God was offering him.

Aloysius could not have hit the target more accurately in this second part of his discourse. The youths listening to him well understood the examples he used; he was, indeed, speaking their language. Furthermore, each of the nobles present sensed that Aloysius was an obvious "doer" rather than a mere "hearer" of the Word. They likewise knew that before them stood one who had eminently practiced what he was preaching. Serving God as a Jesuit was more important to Aloysius than being Marquis of Castiglione. Contemporary authors record that Aloysius' discourse was so well received by the youths that several of them had subsequently sought admission into the Society of Jesus or other religious orders.

This discourse of Aloysius, when read four centuries after it was first delivered, may appear cold and lifeless on the printed page. If we, however, recall that the words flowed from a soul that was totally given to God, uttered by one who was ecstatic in his service of God, and by one who was most eager to share his joy with others, then these words have an eloquence that four centuries can in no way diminish.

This discourse has never had an English version and it is here translated from the Italian for the first time.[7] The material within brackets indicates additions by the translator to facilitate reading, and that in italics indicates Aloysius' use of Latin.

NOTES

1. See V. Cepari, S.J., *Life of Saint Aloysius Gonzaga*, tr. and ed. by F. Goldie, S.J. (Einsiedeln: Benziger, 1891) 182-196, and C. C. Martindale, S.J., *The Vocation of Aloysius Gonzaga* (London: Sheed and Ward, 1929) 168-183.

2. Aloysius twice quotes Saint Catherine's letters in his All Saints sermon which he gave at the Roman College. The date of this discourse is not certain; but it was given while he was a theologian, and therefore either in November 1588, before he left (September 1589) to go to Castiglione, or in November 1590 after his return to Rome.

3. A. Pruvost, S.J., *Oeuvres de S. Louis de Gonzague* (Paris: Casterman, 1862), 82. Collections of Aloysius' letters and spiritual writings have appeared in German, French, and Italian; the best introduction to these various writings, however, is that given by Pruvost.

4. L. Bosio, *Mostra Iconografica Aloisiana settembre-ottobre 1968* (Castiglione delle Stiviere, 1968), 205. The autograph is a paper of twenty-four by thirty centimeters (about eight by twelve inches) and has writing on both sides. Pruvost (p. 83) says that in 1862 it was kept in the church of S. Eufemia in Brescia, and E. Rosa, S.J., (*Lettere ed altri scritti di S. Luigi Gonzaga* [Florence: Editrice Fiorentina, 1926] 161), says that it was still there in 1926. How it got to S. Eufemia is not known; it is presumed that it may have been kept at the Jesuit college in Brescia, and at the time of the Society's suppression in 1773, was given S. Eufemia.

5. Aloysius also quotes Saint Bernard eight times in his All Saints sermon.

6. Cepari, 129 and 233; Martindale, 229.

7. The text used as the basis for this translation is that in P. Bosio Boz, *Lettere e opere spirituali di San Luigi Gonzaga* (Editrice A.V.E., 1949), 118-122.

Following is the essence of the discourse at the Jesuit College, reconstructed from St. Aloysius' notes:

[I]

God speaks to the soul in three ways:

First, by secret inspirations (*Saint Bernard treats of this manner of speaking in his thirty-second sermon on the Canticle* [of Canticles], *where he speaks of the difference between our souls' thoughts and those of God*[1]).

With regard to this manner of speaking, the same Saint says (*fifth sermon of Advent*), that it is secret: "*I have hidden your words in my heart, that I may not sin against you*" [Ps. 119:11], and how we ought to keep them and not merely remember them: "*knowledge puffs one up* [1 Cor. 8:1], *but* [keep them] *as bread is preserved. For God's Word is a living bread and the food of the soul; as long as bread is kept in the cupboard, it can be stolen by a thief, nibbled by a mouse, and can grow stale. So also with God's Word, etc. Take it, therefore, into your stomachs and let it pass on to your affections and your way of life.*"[2] This is what Saint James [1:22] says: "*Be doers*" [of the Word and not merely hearers]. We read in Exodus [16:19-20] that the manna "*not kept as food for the sabbath*" went bad.[3] It is the same with God's Word; it goes bad when it is kept for a purpose other than "*nourishment.*"

The second way: God speaks in Scripture, by means of the prophets in the Old Testament and through Christ in the New. Thus Saint Gregory teaches, (*Book three on First Kings*),[4] and Scripture confirms this when it says: "*The Lord has often spoken to the fathers through the prophets, but in these final days He speaks through His Son*" [see Heb. 1:1-2]. It is of this Word that Saint James says "*Be doers.*" Indeed, it is of little advantage for a Christian to have the privilege of possessing Holy Scripture if he does not live in conformity to it. It is of little advantage to him to have the commandments that God gave in the Old Law [Ex. 20:1-17] if he does not live in conformity to them; it counts little to know the beatitudes that Christ explained in his Sermon on the Mount [Matt. 5:3-12] if one, etc.; it is of little value to know the methods of prayer if one etc.; it is worth little to know in what perfection consists if one is given to imperfection. Furthermore, for such men, Scripture only serves as a letter in their hands which contains their death sentence, as it happened to Uriah, when David sent him to Joab [2 Sam. 11:4].

Third: God speaks through His favors. Thus Saint Bernard, in his forty-fifth sermon on the Canticle, on the words *"How beautiful you are"* [1:14], searches [to explain] the way that God speaks to the soul and the soul to God. *"The speech of the Word,"* he says, *"is loving kindness, that of the soul is the love of devotion."*[5] *And so*, he says further on, *"the speech of the Word is the infusion of grace, the soul's response is thanksgiving."*[6] With regard to this word, the Apostle says *"Be hearers and doers."* We ought not to be content with being merely hearers, but doers, because we must not only occupy ourselves in acknowledging God's favors, which is hearing His Word, but it is necessary for us to return them to the same God, which is *"doing His Word etc."*

We know that all springs have their origin in the sea and that they return to it. *"The Lord Jesus Christ is the sea of all virtue and knowledge"* (*Canticle, first sermon*). *"From him comes the power to be pure in body, diligent in affection and upright in will. Nor is this all. From him too come subtlety of intellect, splendor of eloquence, urbanity of bearing."*[7] It is to him, therefore, that all gifts are to return, for just as water that does not return to the sea but stands in lagoons becomes fetid, so also the gifts of God, health, strength, talent, and eloquence. Those members of the Academy[8] should especially offer their talents, as Saint Augustine exhorts the young Licentius when he says *"If you found a golden chalice, etc."*[9]

[II]

By these three ways you have heard how God speaks to the soul and how we ought do what He tells us. It is worth our while to consider why we ought to do it and with what great care.

A reason, which seems sufficient to me, is the fact that God has spoken. It was enough for God to say that the world should be created for it to be made; will that not suffice for us to reform our lives and walk as He wishes?

Tell me, please, if your Grand Duke,[10] whom you are awaiting and who is soon to arrive, had ordered some poor or rich man of this city to be brought to him, and promised to make him his adopted son and sharer in his kingdom as befits an only son by nature; and if he promised, as long as he should live, to care for him as his own son, and after his death to leave his estates to him as his inheritance, demanding no other condition but that he live and behave as befits his son, namely, that he leave the hovel where he lived and enter his splendid palace, and that he set aside his old rags and dress himself in elegant clothes as becomes such a son, and that he give up the manners and customs that were his as a person of low birth and take on the manners and customs of a person of high birth as the son of the Grand Duke, who of you would be satisfied with hearing this offer and not accepting it immediately?

Now the God of blessings is happy to receive anyone whomever as His son, and promises him such a fatherly providence in this world, that He will never forget us, as Isaiah [49:15-16] says: "*Is it possible* [for a mother to forget her infant and be without tenderness for the child of her womb?] *Even should she forget, I will never forget you. Upon the palms of my hands I have written your name*," and after this life an inheritance as Saint Augustine remarks when commenting on the words "*He gives sleep to his beloved; behold, children are the heritage of the Lord, the fruit of the womb is a reward*" [Ps. 127:2-3].[11] He asks nothing else of us but that we abandon the poor dwelling of our kinsmen and of our mothers, either in affection or in reality, according to each one's calling, and that we live in the royal palace of the King of Heaven, where God is master and the angels are His ministers. He wants us to despoil ourselves of the vile clothing of self-love, and to robe ourselves in charity. He wants us to abandon [the practices] of common and low-born people, which are imperfections and sins, and adopt the practices of the children of God, which are meekness, piety, justice, religion, and the other virtues.

Who of us will be satisfied with hearing this invitation and not accept it, agree to this offer and not carry it out? Certainly, it seems to me that it cannot be for any other reason than the fact that he does not understand God's Word and does not realize what God is promising us.

Aristotle, in the tenth book of his *Ethics*, proves, with many reasons, that spiritual delights are greater than those of the flesh.[12] He then asks the reason why we do not seek them and says that it is because we do not understand them. He gives the example[13] of a king's son who, while still an infant and because he does not know his paternal inheritance, places more value on his nurse's milk or on an apple that a servant has just given him than on his inheritance. He knows one but not the other. But when he grows to maturity you will see that he will soon disdain the milk and the other things, and will strive to obtain his inheritance. And so we too, because we do not realize *"What God has prepared for those who love Him"* [1 Cor. 2:9], have greater appreciation for the nurse's milk, which is consolation, kinsmen, father, mother, all according to the flesh, and greater esteem for an apple of this world than the inheritance of our home, which is the glory of paradise and the benefits which Christ promises to those who follow Him. May it please God that we arrive at that maturity when we will be able to esteem all things according to their proper weight and value, and realize that the grandeur and honor of our own house and all that the world promises us are vile and worthless in comparison to what God promises us.14 *"I will raise you above the heights of the earth"* [Isa. 58:14]. *Refer to what Saint Gregory has to say on this passage.*15

NOTES

1. *S. Bernardi opera*, ed. J. Leclercq, *et al.*, (Rome: Editiones Cistercienses, 1957-1968), vol. 1, pp, 226-233, especially #5, p. 229. Bernard describes the difference between human and divine thinking in this way: "Our own thoughts bear a very close resemblance to the words Truth speaks within us; no one can easily differentiate between what springs from the heart and what he hears from without unless he attends carefully to what the Lord says in the Gospel: 'Out of the heart come evil thoughts' [Matt. 15:19]. . . . So when we yield our hearts to wicked thoughts, the thoughts are our own; if we think on good things, it is God's word. Our hearts produce the evil thoughts, they listen for those that are good. . . . God accordingly utters words of peace, of goodness, of righteousness within us; we do not think these things of ourselves, we hear them in our interior. On the other hand, murders, adulteries, robberies, blasphemies and similar evils come forth from the heart [Matt. 15:19]; we do not hear them, we produce them" (*The Works of Bernard of Clairvaux. On the Song of Songs*, tr. Kilian

Walsh, O.C.S.O., [Kalamazoo: Cistercian Publications, 1976], vol. 2, pp. 137-138).

2. Aloysius here abbreviates what he found in Bernard's fifth sermon for Advent (*Opera*, vol. 4, p. 189, #2). Bernard's exact words are: "Shall we say that it is enough to preserve the memory of them? But to those who keep them in this way the Apostle gives warning that mere 'knowledge puffs up.' Besides, the records of memory are so easily blotted out by oblivion. Keep the word of God in the same way in which the food of your body can be best preserved; for it is a living bread and the food of your soul. Material bread, while it is kept in the cupboard may be stolen by thieves, or nibbled by mice, or may become stale and unfit for us. But once it has been assimilated, we have nothing further to fear from such possibilities. It is thus we should keep the word of God, for 'blessed are they who keep it' [Lk. 11:28] so. Receive this spiritual bread, therefore, into the stomach of your minds, and having been there properly digested, let it be transmitted then to the affections and the will" (*Saint Bernard's Sermons for the Seasons and Principal Festivals of the Year* [Westminster, Md.: Carroll, 1950], vol. 1, pp. 41-42).

With regard to the manna Moses told the Israelites (Ex. 16:19-24): "Let no one keep any of it until tomorrow morning." But there were those who would not obey and "when some kept a part of it over until the following morning it became wormy and rotten," and Moses was displeased with them. Then "on the sixth day, they gathered twice as much food." When Moses was informed of this fact he said "That is what the Lord prescribed. Tomorrow is a day of complete rest, the sabbath, sacred to the Lord . . . whatever is left put away and keep for the morrow." When they "put it away for the morrow, as Moses commanded, it did not become rotten or wormy" (New American Bible translation).

4. This is Gregory's commentary (Book 3, chap. 1, #8) on 1 Samuel 3:4-5 (*PL* 79:148). Gregory here only speaks of the fathers of the Old Testament and says that they "did not speak of themselves, but through them God spoke what He wanted; what is heard in the Scriptures is acknowledged as the voice of God." Since the principle here proposed is a general principle, Aloysius extends it to the New Testament as well. It is also very probable that Aloysius had in mind

the very first words of #9: "God at times speaks through Scripture and at times through secret inspirations." This latter text thus may have given Aloysius the first two divisions of the first part of this exhortation.

5. *Opera*, vol. 2, p. 54, #7. With regard to the manner how the Word and the soul converse, Bernard writes: "So whenever you hear or read that the Word and the soul converse together, and contemplate each other, do not imagine them speaking with human voices nor appearing in bodily form. Listen, this is rather what you must think about it: The Word is a spirit, the soul is a spirit; and they possess their own mode of speech and mode of presence in accord with their nature. The speech of the Word is loving kindness, that of the soul, the fervor of devotion. The soul without devotion is a speechless infant that can never enjoy such intercourse with the Word" (*On the Song of Songs*, vol. 2, p. 238).

6. *Opera*, vol. 2, p. 55, #8: "When the Word therefore tells the soul, 'You are beautiful,' and calls it friend, he infuses into it the power to love, and to know it is loved in return. And when the soul addresses him as beloved and praises his beauty, she is filled with admiration for his goodness and attributes to him without subterfuge or deceit the grace by which she loves and is loved. The Bridegroom's beauty is his love of the bride, all the greater in that it existed before hers. Realizing then that he was her lover before he was her beloved, she cries out with strength and ardor that she must love him with her whole heart and with words expressing deepest affection. The speech of the Word is an infusion of grace, the soul's response is wonder and thanksgiving" (*On the Song of Songs*, vol. 2, p. 238).

7. Though Aloysius states that this is from Bernard's first sermon on the Canticle of Canticles, the quotation is actually from sermon 13 (*Opera*, vol. 1, p. 68, #1). Bernard's words are: "Just as the sea is the ultimate source of wells and rivers, so Christ the Lord is the ultimate source of all virtue and knowledge. . . . Hence from him as from a wellhead comes the power to be pure in body, diligent in affection, and upright in will. Nor is this all. From him too come subtlety of intellect, splendor of eloquence, urbanity of bearing; from him, knowledge and words of wisdom" (*On the Song of Songs*, vol. 1, p. 87).

8. In Jesuit colleges, an academy was a group of students of

superior ability who, under the direction of one of their masters, formed a group to do extra work in connection with one of the subjects which they were then studying. For example, the Virgil Academy read more of the Roman poet than was required for the regular course. Rules for these academies were inserted into the 1599 Jesuit code of education known as *Ratio Studiorum* (cf. *Ratio atque Institutio Studiorum Societatis Iesu [1586 1591 1599]* edited by L. Lukacs, S.J. [Rome: Institutum Historicum Societatis Iesu, 1986], pp. 448-454). The students hearing this exhortation were members of one or another academy, and Aloysius is urging them that because of the gifts they received from God they must return the same to Him.

9. Augustine, *Ep. 26 Ad Licentium*, #6 (*PL* 33:107): "If you found a golden chalice on the ground, you would give it to God's Church. You have received from God talents which are spiritually as valuable as gold and you are using them to indulge your passions; by doing this you are delivering yourself to Satan."

10. This is Ferdinand I, Grand Duke of Tuscany, son of Cosimo I and brother of Francis I. Ferdinand was soon to pay a visit to the Jesuit college in Siena. Pius IV made Ferdinand a cardinal on January 6, 1563, when the latter was only fourteen; at age twenty Ferdinand moved to Rome but never took Holy Orders. At the time when Aloysius was in Florence, a page at the Medici court of Francis I (December 1577 — November 1579), Ferdinand was living in Rome. Upon the death of Francis in 1587, Ferdinand renounced (November 28, 1588) his cardinal's purple and succeeded his brother as Grand Duke.

11. *Ennar. in Ps*. 126 #7-8 (*PL* 37:1672-1673). There is an element of ambiguity as to what Augustine really means; cf. A. Pruvost, *Oeuvres de S. Louis de Gonzague* (Paris: Casterman, 1862), p. 94, n. 1.

12. Aristotle teaches in his *Nicomachean Ethics* (Book 10, chap. 7 [1177a]), "we think happiness has pleasure mingled with it, but the activity of philosophic wisdom is admittedly the pleasantest of virtuous activities (R. McKeon [ed.], *Basic Works of Aristotle* [New York: Random House, 1941] p. 1104). Thomas Aquinas refers to this passage (*Summa Theologica*, 1-2, q. 31, a. 5, *sed contra*) when he writes: "The Philosopher says, in his X *Ethics*, that 'the greatest pleasure comes from the exercise of wisdom.' "

13. The example given here, with all its details, is not found in the tenth book of Aristotle's *Ethics*. Perhaps Aloysius is developing the example given in chap. 3 of book 10 (1174a), where Aristotle notes: "No one would choose to live with the intellect of a child throughout his life, however much he were to be pleased at the things that children are pleased at. . . ." (*Basic Works of Aristotle*, p. 1097).

14. The words "vile and worthless . . . God promises us" are lacking in the original, but seem to be demanded by the sense and are found in extant copies of this exhortation.

15. In the exposition of Job 39:27 in his *Moralia in Iob* (*Corpus Christianorum Series Latina* 143/B, [Turnhout, 1985], #96, p. 1617), Gregory quotes Isaiah 58:14 and then adds: "The heights of the earth are material gains, flattery of subordinates, abundant wealth, honor, and high dignities, everything that the man who still walks in the realm of base desires regards as exalted because he endows them with greatness. But once the heart is attached to heavenly things one soon sees how contemptible is all that once seemed exalted."

VII

The Birds of La Mancha

Cornelia Jessey

When Don Quixote was dying — "restored at last to his right mind" — he said to those around him: "In last year's nests there are no birds this year. I was mad, now I am in my senses. I was Don Quixote of La Mancha; I am now, as I said, Alonso Quixano the Good."[1]

His words have been repeated through the centuries. "In last year's nests there are no birds this year." They bespeak a broken dream, and even in our late twentieth century, a famous writer of spirited theological and carnally human novels recently quoted the words, signifying yet again that the hopes and dreams of the human spirit are, to the world, a madness.

I am referring to Graham Greene's novel *Monsignor Quixote* (New York: Simon & Schuster, 1982). The book was made into a film with Alec Guiness as Don Quixote and Leo McKern as Sancho Panza. In Greene's retelling of the story, the old knight is a parish priest, Father Quixote, who explains to a visiting Bishop that his ancestor was Don Quixote. The story opens with Father Quixote asking the Bishop about the immortal soul in animals. Does Rocinante have a horse soul?

"Where would our faith be if there were not mysteries?" says the visiting Bishop. He means to reward the humble priest for fixing his car and serving him a good dinner by making him a Monsignor. As he leaves, he calls out to Don Quixote (quoting Cervantes): "There are no birds this year in last year's nests."

It was his right mind that made Don Quixote despair of all his knightly ideals. When he was mad with love of the great vision, he knew, as do all bird-watchers, that birds often return to last year's nests.

Outside my window, the scarlet-throated linnets are busy repairing last year's nest under the eaves; the mockingbirds are doing the same thing in the date palm tree. They return to make new life.

Don Quixote returned to last year's nest when he reached up to take Father Pedro de Rivadeneira's *Life of The Blessed Father Ignatius de Loyola* off his bookshelf. The book had appeared in Spanish in 1583) twenty-two years before Cervantes' story came out. Miguel de Unamuno, in *The Life of Don Quixote and Sancho, Expounded with Comment* (Alfred A. Knopf, New York, 1927), writes:

> It was one of the books in the library of Don Quixote, who had read it ere it was so undeservedly flung into the fire in the backyard, after the examination held by the priest and the barber. They had not noticed it among the rest; for if he had, the priest would have done it due reverence and placed it on his head in token thereof. And that he did not notice it is well proved by the fact that Cervantes does not mention it.[2]

The saints of all the ages are contemporaneous, present here and now. The nests made by these high-flying birds, we return to in each new generation. Those elected to return reinforce the old nests, to make a place to create new life. Early in the twentieth century, Unamuno returned to the book Cervantes had written about Don Quixote, to write his own version. A few decades later, near the end of the twentieth century, Graham Greene read Unamuno's version and was inspired to write his own.

"These are not books, lumps of lifeless paper, but *minds* alive on the shelves," said Gilbert Highet. The story of the old knight of La Mancha belongs not only to Cervantes and the readers of his century, but to Unamuno and to Graham Greene and the readers of our century. The ideal of a divine reality to be reached through works for the Good, in the continual war between good and evil, will always be a vision returned to with new life, reborn, to speak in the language of the present.

2. The old knight errant, Don Quixote, is one with the saints in the great literature of divinely-motivated beings who hit upon the strange notion of going into the world to do good:

In short, his wits being quite gone, he hit upon the strangest notion that ever madman hit upon: To put into practice all that he had read of as being the usual practices of knights-errant: righting every wrong, exposing himself to peril and danger.[3]

Unamuno had the inspiration to write his story of Don Quixote with a counterpoint, a hero, a saint from historical reality — Ignatius de Loyola. He introduces them both in their likenesses as hidalgos, Spanish gentlemen, and with Don Quixote's fiery temper:

Of this same temperament was also that knight of Christ, Ignatius de Loyola, of whom we shall have much to say; of him his biographer Father Pedro de Rivadeneira tells us . . . that he was of a very hot and irascible temperament.[4]

Chrysogonus Waddell, in a brilliant essay on early Cistercian hagiography, compares hagiography to iconography. He tells how the icon "has nothing to do with photographic realism, but functions rather as a means of making the divine reality effectively present to the believer."

Czeslaw Milosz wrote, with similar insight, that "the work of human thought should be to withstand the test of brutal naked reality; if it cannot, it is worthless." Unamuno catches all this up in a single ray of light, the perception that divine reality is The Good. He writes:

God awakes for those that are good. . . . May it be that we, poor dreams that dream, can dream that which is man's watch in thine eternal vigil, O God? What if goodness be the watchman's light? . . . "For even in dreams / Good deeds are never lost."[5]

For divinely-motivated beings, Goodness expresses the divine reality, as Saint Francis of Assisi wrote: "You are what is good, all that is good, the supreme good, true and living Lord God."

So thought Don Quixote, whose obedience to the will of God was so perfect "it never occurred to him to consider whether or not the imminent adventure was suitable." He sought honor and glory in the name of God.

> The root of thine intense desire not to die was thy goodness, my Don Quixote. The good is not resigned to disintegration; it feels that goodness partakes of the nature of God, of that God who is the God, not of the dead, but the living, since for His sake all things live.[6]

To be able to read, just as to be able to write, *stories* requires the spirit of imagination. Along with the writer, the reader enters the personal self on the plane of otherness. Everything, the wind, the weather, trees, animals, birds, insects, dogs, cats, angels, witches, babies, the aged, the lovers, rocks, horses, every variety of this varied creation turns into a secret door that opens, for the self to enter the realm of others, without losing one's identity. To go on being always oneself is an intolerable restriction to the spirited imagination. But to be oneself with yesterday's tens of thousands years is to be liberated, the way to personal immortality.

For Ignatius de Loyola as for Don Quixote, books were the fire that ignited the personal self, sending it inward, outward, upward. Thus, writes Unamuno, Don Quixote was trained, tempered, trued:

> It was no fool of a boy throwing himself headlong into an ill-understood career, but a sensible, intelligent man becoming crazed by sheer maturity of spirit.[7]

His story begins as the old knight sallies forth unseen by the back gate.

> Does this sally not remind you of another knight, of the Company of Jesus, Ignatius de Loyola . . . before conversion an eager reader of profane books of chivalry; yet, after being wounded at Pamplona, when he had read the life of Christ and the lives of saints, began "to experience a change of heart and a wish to imitate . . . what he had read?" And so one morning, heedless of the advice of his brothers, he "set out, accompanied by two servants," and began his life of

adventures in Christ. . . . Father Pedro de Rivadeneira tells us this in chapters i, iii, and x.[8]

Even Don Quixote's going out at night, after arriving at an inn, to watch over his arms in the courtyard, reminds Unamuno of the likeness to Ignatius:

> On Christmas Eve, 1522, he, too, watched his arms at the altar of Our Lady of Montserrat. Listen to Father Tivadeneira. . . "As he had read in books of chivalry that maiden knights used to watch their arms, he, as a maiden knight of Christ, in order spiritually to imitate that knightly rite and to watch his own apparently poor and fragile, but really strong and gorgeous, arms, which he had put on against man's natural enemy, all that night, partly standing and partly kneeling, remained watching before the image of Our Lady, offering himself to her with all his heart, bitterly weeping for his sins and promising to mend his ways thenceforth."[9]

When Don Quixote stops a party of silk merchants and tries to make them confess that in all the world there is no maiden fairer than Dulcinea, and the merchants protest that they have never seen her, Don Quixote insists: "The point is that without seeing her you believe, confirm and swear and maintain it."

Unamuno cries out: "Wonderful knight, who demands of men who are merchants and know only the material kingdom of wealth, to acknowledge the spiritual realm!"

Unamuno admits that there are times when Saint Ignatius is more prudent than Don Quixote. For example, en route to Montserrat, he falls in with a Moor, one of the few remaining in Spain, and they get into a discussion on the virginity and purity of the most glorious Virgin:

> On parting from the Moor, Ignatius was perplexed as to what action to take, whether or not the faith he professed and Christian piety obliged him to hasten to overtake the Moor and stab him for his effrontery and insolence in so shamelessly insulting the ever blessed stainless Virgin. But he came to a crossroad and left the decision to

his horse. God willed that his horse be enlightened and choose, not the road taken by the Moor, but the one best for Ignatius.[10]

Unamuno adds that the existence of the Company of Jesus "is due to an inspired horse."

It is not a cynical remark, simply a scriptural statement, which conforms to a different way of looking at the world. Throughout the Old and New Testament stories, animals appear to be wiser, certainly more psychic, than humans.

Don Quixote, knocked down in his armor and powerless to rise, is helped by a villager and brought home. His niece begs her uncle to stay and not seek adventures that make him appear of unsound mind.

Ignatius, too, was besieged by his brother Martin Garcia de Loyola, "who sought to dissuade his younger brother Ignatius from seeking adventures in Christ, from throwing himself into causes" which only robbed "us of what we expected of you" and "soil our lineage with everlasting . . . dishonor."

3. Unamuno could have mentioned Aloysius Gonzaga as yet another in the knight-errant-of-Christ tradition whose family harassed him, especially his father.

C.C. Martindale, S.J., writing of the princely families of Italy in those times, describes their "tigerish bloodthirstiness," which was combined with abhorrent immorality and an equally savage faith.

Out of this appalling heredity sprang the precocious spiritual genius who was practicing contemplative prayer at age seven, comparable to the musical precocity of Mozart. By age twelve the young prince already perceived that his society could not be reformed from within and determined to enter a religious order. "He was reading the life of Saint Ignatius. Like Ignatius in the early days of his fervor, he piled up his penances and began to flog himself using his dogs' leashes. . . He developed some odd physical mannerisms such as keeping his eyes down, especially with women.[11]

His father depended on him as the eldest son to continue the Gonzaga reign. For Aloysius to dare ask permission to enter a religious order was, to his father, a direct assault upon the power of their house and a dishonor to their station in life. He called in eminent churchmen and laymen to try to persuade his son toward the "normal vocation" in the military, as befitted a princely family.

Further maddening was the young man's choice of the Society of Jesus, an order detested and feared by the worldly powerful because Ignatius de Loyola had gone farther than other religious orders in making their vow of poverty require a promise not to accept ecclesiastical dignities. Though so young, only fifteen, Aloysius was already most knowledgeable about these things. It was no use just becoming a priest. For a member of a princely family, a religious vocation was often just exchanging one form of grandeur for another: "These involved not only elaborate exterior homage, but usually vast revenues; a kinsman of his had been appointed archbishop at eight; made a cardinal at fourteen."[12]

No such preferments were possible for members of the Society of Jesus. Aloysius' family would not be able to keep him from being poor. Ignatius had to assure his brother that his family would not be dishonored.

The similarities of this knight-of-Christ to Don Quixote appears even in their family's contempt for a spiritual vocation. Of course Unamuno finds a few dissimilarities — one that particularly dejects him is in the relationship to women. Don Quixote stresses that no knight-errant can be without his lady, "because it is as natural and proper to be in love as to the heaven to have stars."

The knights of Christ did have their lady whom they loved, the Lady Mary, the greatest star in the heavens, but Don Quixote meant the loving of an everyday woman. Ignatius thought the everyday woman an impediment. When Dona Isabel de Rosell endeavored to form a community of women under the obedience of the Company, Loyola wrote Pope Paul III to exempt the Company from that burden by letters apostolical of May 20, 1547, saying: "It is unsuitable for this least of Companies to have special charge of ladies with a vow of obedience."

Strumpets, on the other hand, were no problem to these knights. Don Quixote was armed a knight by "the two strumpets who girded on him his spurs." Ignatius de Loyola befriended "lost public women," escorting them through the midst of Rome to place them in the convent of Saint Martha, or in the home of some honorable lady,

" 'where they might be instructed in every virtue' (Rivadeneira, Book III, chap ix)."[13]

Both men suffered brutal encounters with the devil. Ignatius, knight-errant-of-Christ, was beaten and choked by the very Devil. Don Quixote, knight-errant of the laity, encountered the devil in the laity, as exemplified in the incident where he frees the galley-slaves, who turn on him, stone him, and take his jacket and Sancho's coat. Severely criticized for freeing such vicious criminals, Quixote says:

> It is no business or concern of knights-errant to inquire whether the afflicted, enchained, or oppressed whom they meet on the highway go that way and suffer as they do because of their faults or because of their fortunes. It concerns them only to aid them, as being in distress and to regard their sufferings, not their crimes.[14]

Unamuno eloquently expands on this theme: "Until at the sight of even the most horrid crime, we learn to exclaim to its doer, 'Poor Brother!' our Christianity will not sink in any deeper than the skin of our souls." When Cervantes tells that Quixote's legs were "far from clean," Unamuno grumbles: "He might have omitted that, especially since personal cleanliness was not typical of knights nor of Spanish gentlemen." Here was another of the differences in Ignatius de Loyola. "Although he loved poverty, neglect of cleanliness displeased him." Cleanliness must not be carried to an extreme, of course, and Ignatius "allotted a rigorous penance to a novice for washing his hands sometimes with soap, regarding that as too dainty for a novice."

Cleanliness was a moral problem, indeed it was all kinds of a problem, physically, and spiritually. There was a dense spiritual confusion about the sanctity of poverty. The distinction between voluntary and involuntary poverty was too subtle. Centuries passed before a more enlightened spirituality saw the distinction: that the Lord Jesus chose to be poor and to live with and serve the poor, not because it was good to be born into slavery or involuntary poverty, but because it was bad. Yet to be born into riches was worse, unless the rich saw the basic principle was sharing. It was a great problem as it is today.

Don Quixote's old wrinkled stockings tear ("Oh, disaster unworthy of such a personage!"). He is distressed, and Cervantes comments on the tragedy of poverty among worthy gentlemen. Unamuno turns to Ignatius to clarify the different kinds of poverty and the significance of the religious vow, and how it not only related to material poverty, but to challenge the spiritual evil of pride, "aware that the most terrible enemy of heroism is the shame of appearing poor." Unamuno continues:

> Poverty is the worst crime of our day. In modern society the classes
> called the most advanced and cultivated are distinguished by their
> hatred of poverty and the poor.[15]

4. It took heroism to accept a vow of poverty; it took heroism to serve the divine vision. Such commitments were considered madness, of which Saint Teresa of Ávila said: "I pray we may all go mad, for love of Him whom they called so, for our sake."

When Don Quixote entered the Cave of Montesinos, he prayed God to aid him and drew his sword, hacking away the brambles, so to enter the abyss, "where he enjoyed astonishing visions."

Cervantes doubts their authenticity and says Don Quixote retracted his visions on his deathbed. Unamuno, possessed of the same hot temper as Ignatius de Loyola and Don Quixote, storms:

> O petty historian, how little thou knowest about visions! Doubtless
> thou didst not read or, as it was published twenty-two years before
> thy publication of the history of Don Quixote, if thou didst read it,
> thou didst not well meditate the book of the *Life of the Blessed
> Father Ignatius de Loyola* by Father Pedro de Rivadeneira, who . . .
> tells us of the visions of the knight-errant-of-Christ and how he saw
> the holy humanness of our Redeemer Jesus Christ and sometimes
> also the most glorious Virgin. . . . Those who mock such visions are
> commonly men who neither know, understand, nor have heard tell
> what the spirit is.[16]

But those who are fired by the immortal vision, even though their eyes have not seen but have only read in books of such things, trust the reality unfolded by Ignatius de Loyola and Don Quixote:

> For if it be given us, at last, as they promise thee, to behold the beatific vision of God, that vision will be a work, a continuous and never-completed conquest of the Truth Supreme and Infinite . . . O Lord . . . let it always cost us effort to attain unto Thee.[17]

The saints experience and communicate the reality that lies behind the temporal. Don Quixote comes up to laborers carrying images wrapped in cloths, carved in relief for an altar screen in their village. He begs to see the figures. The laborers uncover images of Saint George, Saint Martin, Saint James the Moor-slayer, and Saint Paul. Don Quixote cries out:

> I take it as a happy omen, brothers, to have seen what I have; for these saints and knights were of the same profession as myself . . . only there is this difference between them and me, that they were saints and fought with divine weapons, whereas I am a sinner and fight with human ones. They won heaven by force of arms, for heaven suffereth violence; but I, so far, know not what I have won by dint of my sufferings.[18]

Don Quixote's sallying forth into the world is the beginning of the old knight's spiritual evolution, or, to use Unamuno's favorite term, "immortalization." If Don Quixote were to return to the world today, says Unamuno, he would not come a sword-bearing knight-errant but as the good shepherd Quixote. He would be a shepherd of souls and would read books of divine enlightenment:

> What if those books that might be a light to thy soul should send thee off to other, though new, kinds of errantries? Is it not opportune to recall here once more Ignatius de Loyola at Pamplona, wounded in bed, asking to have some books of chivalry . . . and obtaining the Life of Christ our Lord?[19]

Although no miracles are reported after the death of Don Quixote, he is an immortal:

> And if the pious biographer considers Loyola's greatest miracle to be his founding of the Company of Jesus, may we not regard as Don Quixote's greatest miracle the fact that he caused his biography to be written by Cervantes, who in his other works showed the feebleness of his genius... The story was dictated to Cervantes by another man, whom Cervantes harbored within himself, a spirit dwelling in the depths of his soul . . . and I even suspect that while I have been expounding . . . Don Quixote and Sancho have visited me secretly without my knowledge, and uncovered and displayed to me the inmost sanctuary of their hearts. . . . We often regard the writer as a real, genuine, historic person . . . and consider as purely imaginary the characters he portrays in his fictions; the truth is just the contrary: his characters are the realities, the real people, and they make use of him who seems to us of flesh and bone in order to take on form and being . . . there will be many strange things to be seen when we all awake from the dream of life.[20]

5. As Loyola's greatest miracle is the founding of the Company of Jesus, Don Quixote's great miracle is the continuing making-present of divine reality behind our temporal moment, to unbelievers. As our twentieth century draws to a close with neuroses such as "compassion fatigue," and the tireless propaganda of greed as the good life — suddenly — the birds of La Mancha return in Graham Greene's tale of *Monsignor Quixote*.[21]

Father Quixote, a poor parish priest in a dusty Spanish town, having been dubbed Monsignor by a visiting Bishop for fixing his car and giving him dinner, is persuaded by his friend the Communist mayor (Sancho Panza), to wear a sign of his knight-errantry. They set off for Madrid to get him properly outfitted. The old priest is clothed with purple socks and a purple *pechera*. Having got as far as Madrid they decide to go farther. From León, the priest telephones his housekeeper, who warns him not to come home because the local Bishop has replaced him with a young priest and is telling everyone

Father Quixote is mad. However they do return, and when the Bishop says he is going to put the old priest in the madhouse, the Mayor compares Father Quixote's constant reading of the stories of saints with Don Quixote's reading of books of chivalry, saying: "He touches God." Father Quixote has to make a daring escape, with the help of Sancho, but his most precious treasure has been taken from him. His priestly duties have been suspended, and he is forbidden to say Mass. He calls this his "sentence of death here on earth."

They make a pilgrimage to Salamanca to visit the shrine of Unamuno, and the mayor admits he once studied for the priesthood but could not give up his fondness for girls. Father Quixote confesses that he was never tempted by a woman because Thérèse of Lisieux protected him. The mayor says Unamuno kept him in church for years, and his ghost haunts him.

Father Quixote has his own sorrows. He is afraid that if he is incapable of human love, he cannot love God; so he doesn't feel lucky to have escaped temptation and prays to God he may know temptation.

Meanwhile they must avoid the police, so they head for a remote Trappist monastery. En route they go through a town where the priests are utterly corrupted. Father Quixote battles them just as his ancestor attacked the windmills. Like his ancestor, he is knocked down and injured, but able to resume the journey. At last they arrived at the monastery, Saint Benedict Among the Thorns, but the police, the Guardia Civile, are on their heels. The Abbot gives the old priest and the mayor sanctuary, preventing the police from seizing them. Father Quixote is dying and begs to say a Mass. The monk says: "Tomorrow." Poor Father Quixote goes to bed, murmuring: "I have no right to say a Mass. My bishop forbids it."

During the night he rises from sleep in a trance-like state and goes into the church. Sancho follows him, also the abbot and a guest.

There, in the old Latin rite, Monsignor Quixote offers his last Mass, at a bare altar, without vestments. He lifts the invisible chalice and the invisible Host. The abbot and the guest kneel. The priest consumes the invisible bread and drinks the wine from the invisible chalice; then gives communion to all present. He says to the communist mayor: "You must kneel, compañero." He gives him communion. Then the knight-errant dies.

The visiting professor is moved but says: "We saw no bread nor wine."

The abbot responds: "*We* saw no bread nor wine, but *he* did."

The mayor thinks of the Guardia Civile still carrying on the old oppression, and yet Franco the dictator is dead. He sees that the hate of such a man dies with him, but the love of a man like Father Quixote lives after him. "For how long? And to what purpose?"

The poet Rilke was given to see behind the curtain of the visible, the invisible bread and wine, and he wrote in his poem series, the *Duino Elegies*:

> "Someday, emerging at last from this terrifying vision
> May I burst into praise to assenting angels."[22]

The transformation of the visible into the invisible is a terrifying vision, he explained, "only because we, its lovers and transformers, still depend on the visible; all the worlds of the universe are plunging into the invisible, as into their next deepest reality."

Saint Paul understood this folly: "The natural man receives not the things of the Spirit of God, for they are a foolishness unto him" (1 Cor. 2:14).

It is in books we meet Don Quixote and Ignatius de Loyola; Aloysha (Dostoyevsky's ardently burning soul in *The Brothers Karamazov*) and Aloysius Gonzaga; Thérèse Martin and Thomas Merton, and a great multitude of magnetic personalities whose transforming reality changes us.

What is surprising is that we take this for granted. We are the apostles on the road to Emmaus, accepting as everyday encounters meetings that are out of the dimension we call time. Then comes the delayed shock: "Were not our hearts burning within us?" Every day we meet those we take for granted are the real people, yet they are the ones whom we can't remember. "I recall the face but not the name."

When we meet spirit-filled people, the name is of the essence. Without the name Don Quixote, do all the sketches mean anything? To know his face? Does anyone know anyone's real face? Do I know my own? There are no photographs, no paintings from life, no rough sketches from life, of the face of Christ. We only know His name. Yet it is His name that electrifies us, that tells us who He is and charges us with a visible connection which enables us to sense the invisible.

Behind the visible is an invisible reality, behind all our words is the Archetypal Word; behind the music, the Archetypal Sound, the Note. Anyone at any age may hear the Note, may see the invisible behind the visible (a paradox of seeing what eye cannot see). Children may hear and, like Mozart, pour forth prodigies of music; or spiritual wisdom, like Aloysius Gonzaga and Thérèse Martin.

The music of Mozart is for all generations, but Aloysius and Thérèse are up against the limitations of a temporal vocabulary: the devotional words of a religious milieu out of date, unexpressive, trite. Indeed the spiritual vocabulary of Aloysius was shopworn when Thérèse first heard his story read. She encountered him on the narrow ridge, "a tortured boy, grim and scarred from battling" (his father), and was repelled by this sorry knight-errant who walked head down, eyes on the ground. His story did not stress the appalling corruption of his environment: ("No one would now dare print the pictures with which the Gonzaga palaces were adorned.") No wonder Aloysius walked head down. When he finally made it into the religious order of his choice, the Jesuits took that out of him:

> His superiors made him forgo many of the austerities he had
> practiced . . . the master of novices had a stiff pasteboard collar
> made for the youth which compelled him to keep his head in an
> erect position. . . . Aloysius responded with good grace and even
> laughter . . . he to whom laughter had been a strange thing made it a
> matter of merriment when he appeared among his companions with
> his head set in this singular frame.[23]

The book read at table did not mention the laughter. Thérèse said:

> "I do not like Saint Aloysius as much as blessed Théophane Vénard,
> for in the life of the former it was said he was grave and sad even
> during recreation whereas Théophane Vénard was always cheerful,
> although he suffered a great deal."[24]

Perhaps Thérèse could not imagine the corruption of the environment from which Aloysius sprang. The contrast between their backgrounds could not have been greater. Two of his brothers were destined to be murdered, and his mother, six years after the death of her saintly Aloysius, was seized by peasants in revolt, along with her youngest son Diego. They shot the child, who ran to his mother's arms and died; then they stabbed Donna Marta and left her bleeding to death. A citizen picked her up and cared for her. It is said she died happy, seeing her beloved Luigi in a vision. Thérèse, child of devout nineteenth-century middle-class parents, wrote of her childhood: "God has surrounded me with love all my life; the first things I remember are tender smiles and caresses."

Nevertheless, it was Aloysius who imprinted her soul with his mark. Like Don Quixote and Ignatius de Loyola, Thérèse had been an ardent reader of stories of knights-errant. One day in the convent they read a book by Léon Bloy. She recognized Bloy's extreme austerity. It was identical with the passion of Aloysius Gonzaga, which was the passion of Christ. She recognized the spirit of the divine knight-errant. Bloy could be exactly described, like Aloysius, as grim and scarred from battling. "One wonders how such a book happened to find its way into the Carmel of Lisieux," exclaims Hilda Goerres. Indeed Bloy was a painful thorn in the side of the smug middle-class Catholics, whom he scathingly criticized for their selfishness, self-righteousness, and obsessive money-grubbing. Bloy seared them with a loathing comparable to Aloysius' loathing of the ruling class. The middle class had inherited the materialism, the greed and moral vacuum of that ruined nobility. Bloy's preaching of suffering with Christ as the salvation that alone could heal humanity was recognized by Thérèse as identical with Aloysius. She copied lengthy passages out of his writings on the subject of suffering as the gift of divine love.

Aloysius described himself "as a piece of twisted iron needing to be twisted straight," Thérèse used the same image, saying that suffering, the gift of divine love, penetrated her soul "as a fire penetrates iron."

Her words about the shower of roses come from Aloysius, and his presence was strongly with her as she lay dying. Rebuked by one of the sisters for declaring she would soon die (the sister had said: "You have not yet worked long enough"), Thérèse said: "Look at Saint Aloysius. God could have made him live long and evangelize nations, but He did not choose to do so, because He destined him to a more fruitful mission than if he had lived to be eighty."

These high-flying birds returned to Aloysius Gonzaga's old nest to reinforce and make strong cradles for the new life it was their mission to bring: to break down walls within the Church and open to the world the hidden wholeness of the Christ spirit.

This lark-like girl Thérèse was given to make space for the modern suffering of despair, as a valid suffering which spiritual souls had to know. She was the first of the modern saints who understood the weakness, the despair, the long dark night of psychological confession as the very work of the modern human soul; no heroic stoicism:

> "Let us suffer, if necessary without courage. Jesus suffered many things in sadness. Without sadness, how can the soul be said to suffer? . . . We would like to suffer generously, in the grand manner! What a delusion . . . we must learn to suffer without courage, feebly and with sadness."[25]

She was opening church doors to the age of the laity, for it is the laity that suffer without courage.

This was the way of Don Quixote, the knight-errant of the laity. He suffered many things in sadness, without courage, feebly, as when he was knocked down and couldn't get up again, or when he was arrested for freeing the galley-slaves and put in a cage:

> Shut up in a coop and carried in an oxcart . . . he leaned against the bars, as silent and patient as if he were not a man of flesh . . . as of course he was not, but a man of spirit . . . a canon came along bent on proving to him that there never were knights-errant in the world. The canon failed to convince Don Quixote.[26]

Unamuno says it would have been impossible to do so, for the very reason given by Saint Teresa for the failure of preachers to make sinners leave their evil ways: "Because the preachers have a great deal of sense and have not lost it, as the apostles lost it in the great fire of the love of God."[27]

NOTES

1. Miguel de Cervantes, *Don Quixote* (New York: The Heritage Press, n.d.), p. 315.

2. Miguel de Unamuno, *The Life Of Don Quixote and Sancho* (New York: Knopf, 1927), p. 5.

3. Cervantes, op. cit., p. 54.

4. Unamuno, op. cit. p. 6.

5. Ibid., p. 322.

6. Ibid., p. 312.

7. Ibid., p. 8.

8. Ibid., p. 13.

9. Ibid., p. 22.

10. Ibid., p. 30.

11. C. C. Martindale, S.J., *The Vocation of Aloysius Gonzaga* (New York: Sheed & Ward, 1945), p. 74.

12. Ibid., p. 94.

13. Unamuno, op. cit., p. 61.

14. Ibid., p. 109.

15. Ibid., p. 221.

16. Ibid., p. 187.

17. Ibid., p. 212.

18. Ibid., p. 244.

19. Ibid., p. 294.

20. Ibid., p. 324.

21. Graham Greene, *Monsignor Quixote* (New York: Simon & Schuster, 1982).

22. Rainer Maria Rilke, *Duino Elegies* (New York: W.W. Norton, 1939), p. 79

23. Martindale, op. cit., p. 88.

24. Ida Goerres, *The Hidden Face* (New York: Pantheon, 1959) p. 307.

25. Ibid., p. 329.

26. Unamuno, op. cit., p. 137.

27. Ibid., p. 143.

Additional sources: Czeslaw Milosz, *The Collected Poems*, 1931-1987 (Ecco Press, 1988) has been of inspiration in the work undertaken, as has Chrysogonus Waddell, *The Exegetical Challenge of Early Cistercian Hagiography* (Cistercian Studies, V. XXI, 1986: 3, p 195). I also wish to thank Father Herbert Palmer, O.S.B., Librarian of the Prince of Peace Abbey Library, Oceanside, California, for his valuable help in locating the books I needed for my research.

VIII

Aloysius Mystic?

M. Basil Pennington, O.C.S.O.

Authors devote many pages of their study of mystical theology to listing and analyzing the various phenomena: levitation, locutions, insensibility, etc.[1] And it is these phenomena that have, of course, "made the news." So much so that when we hear the word mystic we immediately think of them and expect the mystic to be, if not flying, at least insensitive to the pinpricks of everyday life. The fact is the mystic is probably more sensitive to these, especially as they afflict others, for the essence of mysticism lies elsewhere.

I will be ever grateful for a little book put out many years ago by Father Gabriel Diefenbach: *Common Mystic Prayer.*[2] Today I would want to rewrite the book in many respects, but when I first came upon it the experience was for me a breakthrough moment. Diefenbach quotes and makes his own the lament of E. I. Watkin that

> mysticism should still be so widely regarded with suspicion even by Catholic writers, as something abnormal, something with which the healthy religion of normal folk has no concern. Or at best it is considered an extraordinary favor, granted like miracle working to a few chosen souls, with which the ordinary Catholic has nothing to do. Yet mysticism is the very lifeblood of sanctity.[3]

As these authors go on to point out, mysticism is not something accidental to our life in Christ but "belongs to the supernatural life of sanctifying grace and is organically connected with it."[4]

God the Father and God the Son and God the Holy Spirit were completely happy. From all eternity They were having a wonderful time, or a wonderful eternity, just filled with joy. Well, you know that when we are filled with joy and are very happy, we want very much to share it. And that is precisely why God made us, to share Their joy.[5] But there was a problem.

Let me be a little whimsical here. I have a wonderful little dog, pure mongrel. Each morning after Mass I go out for a walk, and my little friend runs up to me, jumps up and kisses me, slobbering my beard, and then bounds down the road ahead of me. We are great friends. But when I am very happy and want to share my joy, I don't usually go out to the dog house, sit down and say, "Well, ol' friend, guess what!" No. I look for one of my brothers, because I need someone who is at my level and can enter into my human joy. Now, suppose my fairy godmother comes along and with her magic wand bops my little dog over the head and he becomes human. She would still have to endow him with human faculties, so that he could think as I think and feel as I feel — then he could enter into my joy.

There is a greater distance between you and me and God than there is between you and me and my little dog. So what did God do? He did not bop us over the head but dunked us into the water. We went into the waters human and came out human plus. We were made partakers of Their divine nature and life. We were divinized. This is the supernatural life. It is super. It is above our original created nature. It does not obliterate that nature. It leaves it fully intact. Indeed, it begins the process by which our created nature is fully restored to its pristine beauty and magnificence. Still, we need faculties that correspond to our new participated nature. We need to be able to know as God knows and experience as They experience. Thus, at baptism we are given, besides the theological virtues which enable our natural faculties to reach beyond themselves, a new set of faculties consonant with our new nature. These faculties are called the gifts of the Holy Spirit: "gifts" because they are freely given; "of the Holy Spirit" because it is the Holy Spirit, who is given to us at baptism to be our spirit, who acts through them. Through the gifts we can begin to know as God knows and experience as God experiences, see things and act in the way God would. We can truly enter into the divine joy. Our faith, hope, and love are vivified by the experiential. This activity of the Holy Spirit in us through the gifts of the Holy Spirit is the mystic life. The gifts are given to everyone of the baptized. We are thus all called to be mystics.

No one knows us as well as God knows us, They who created us. And no one respects us as They do. God knows that the greatest thing about us is our freedom, for herein lies our power to love. And God is love. We have all received the gifts of the Holy Spirit, all of us who have been baptized. And the Spirit dwells within us. Nonetheless, we are free to leave these gifts all wrapped up and to function solely with our rational intellect and will, at the purely human level. We can through faith open our minds to the revelation that points beyond and reach out to what or who is revealed with that we call charity. And in this our essential holiness lies. And we can open our minds and hearts to allow the Spirit of God to bring us into experiential knowledge and love of the Divine.

The mystic is the one who allows the Holy Spirit to act in his or her life through the gifts of the Holy Spirit received at baptism. Our role in the mystical life lies in allowing the Spirit the freedom to act. The role of the ascetical life, which is not wholly prior but indeed concomitant with the mystical life, is to free ourselves from what prevents us from allowing the Spirit to act in us: the domination of our false self with its projects, its possessions and its self-centeredness. Unfortunately our ascetic practice can become a project in itself and end up binding us instead of freeing us.

Was Aloysius a mystic? Yes, indeed. And all the asceticism which was so evident in his life may have been necessary so that this very sensitive young man of proud noble lineage and upbringing could be free to allow the Spirit of God to act freely within him through the gifts he had received, like the rest of us, at baptism.

Aloysius' extreme asceticism is difficult to understand, especially for the modern. It has to be remembered that not even the saints were infallible. They made mistakes. Also, though they may have been considered saints during their lifetime, in fact they were still saints in the making — not finished products. Aloysius certainly overdid it and severely injured his health. Unlike Saint Bernard, whom Aloysius admired deeply and read much, Aloysius did not live long enough to regret his youthful excesses. Indeed his ardent longing for death, which probably had something to do with his early demise, was something of an excess. But God works through our folly, uses it, brings out his purpose: "For those who love God all things work together unto good" (Rom. 8:28).

We certainly see signs of the activity of the Holy Spirit acting through the gifts in the life of our saint. The spiritual insight and determination he showed at a very precocious age were undoubtedly the fruit of the activity of the gifts of knowledge, understanding, and fortitude as well as of counsel. It took a spirit-filled fortitude for the young nobel to remain faithful to his resolve to become a religious at the age of seventeen in the face of much opposition, to be tough in the face all the challenges the religious life offered this naturally delicate and physically weakened young man, and in the end to give himself to ministering to the plague victims at the conscious risk of his life.

For me, this is the gift that stands out most in the life of Aloysius: his fortitude. But the other gifts were active. His piety or filial devotion is total. He really did, like his divine Master, seek always to do the things that pleased the Father. There was a deep reverential fear of offending God, to the extent that might seem to us more coarse sinners to border on the scrupulous.

He certainly showed the discernment that comes from the gift of counsel. He was very clear on his vocation and on how to live it. One of my favorite stories about him is this: One day as they played cards at recreation, one of the pious novices raised the hypothetical question (as novices are wont to do): What would you do now if you knew you were going to die in five minutes. Aloysius is reported as stating: I would go right on playing cards. God is where his will is. He won't be found elsewhere. And that is where he wants to find us, not only at the moment of our death, but all the time. The activity of the this gift was also evident in the way the young religious was able to enter into "worldly" affairs and act as an effective mediator in family disputes.

But what in Aloysius would most appeal to today's young men and women? He has been hailed as the patron of youth. There must be something besides his early death that justifies such a title.

Probably it is not the exaggerated asceticism he practiced, especially during his last years as a lay person. The discipline of religious life, with its obedience to the directives of superiors, brought this somewhat into moderation. Perhaps we can best understand young Aloysius if we see in his undertakings the exaggerations of one in love. He had come to passionately love our Lord — herein lay his essential holiness — and his times told him this was the way to show one's love for our Lord. He was a man of his own times. When God said to Solomon, Ask what I shall give you, Solomon answered, An understanding heart — an answer that much pleased God. When Jesus said the same to Thomas Aquinas, his reply was: Nothing, Lord, but you — a beautiful response that must have pleased our Lord very much. But the response of John of the Cross, Aloysius' contemporary was: Only to suffer more for you, O Lord. Devotion to Christ's Passion was one of the principle devotions of Aloysius. Perhaps he had some special insight into those words of Saint Paul: To fill up what is wanting in the passion of Christ (Col. 1:24). Certainly Aloysius was not canonized or set up as the patron of youth for having destroyed his health or for having beaten himself till he bled. He was canonized, he was truly a saint, because of his great love. And this love was in the maturing Aloysius expressed in ways that are more attractive to us today.

A rich young man, gifted in many ways, who freely gives up his princedom and all the possibilities that offered to follow a vision, an ideal, and to enter into a life of service of his fellow humans — that is attractive. Though it might be more attractive if Aloysius had done it at a more mature age, and with more human struggle, than at such an early age and so surely under the instinct of the Holy Spirit. What is perhaps more attractive is the way this young student, who could have stayed safely with his books and his fellow students and all his scholastic activities, nonetheless went out to serve and to seek to alleviate the sufferings of the most wretched and seemingly repulsive victims of the plague. And in so doing, knowingly and willingly placed his own life, with all its promise, in jeopardy, the realness of which his subsequent death confirmed. This is admirable heroism. This is the stuff that inspires. And it was done and lived by a fellow student. Without any great theatrics, but with a quietness and peace, a certain matter-of-factness. It comes across then as a heroism that is accessible: If a guy like Aloysius can do it, I can do it.

And it is needed today, even down to detail. The Book of Revelation tells of the four horsemen riding across the world spreading their terrible scourges: war, famine, plague, and death. We certainly have had war. Hunger has been the cruel slaughterer in many parts of our world. Death comes to us all. But with modern medicine, plague seemed absent until quite recently. Now it is claiming young lives by the thousands. In the United States this plague has been largely associated with a kind of activity which has been labeled perverted, and its victims have received much less of the care and compassion due them. In many cases they have even been abandoned by their families, their own mothers and fathers. And those who care for them, while not so exposed to infection by the disease, are usually socially tainted by the association, especially young men. Where would Aloysius be in the face of this plague? He is a role model here.

Sin was not important to Aloysius — unlike some other saints and like too much of the Church thinking of our time. He may well never have sinned, at least in the way theologians have defined as "mortal." If he had, he would no doubt have been profoundly aware of it and its horror. But it would not have become a great life issue for him. He would simply have confessed it, with deepest sorrow, and received absolution, receiving God's full forgiveness and forgiving himself, and then gotten on with life. For him, what certainly did matter, what was central in his thinking and outlook, was the demands of love. And he was ever more conscious in how he fell away from these, the demands of a love that is so great that it is God Himself. In this he had no difficulty in identifying himself with all us sinners. We all fall away from the demands of the divine love. The important thing then is not our sin but the love. Realizing this all young men and women can identify with Aloysius. Our sinfulness does not distance us from him. His reported innocence need not either. We all share the sin of distancing ourselves from the demands of an immensely loving God. Aloysius was exquisitely aware of this in himself and walks with us in our sin. What he urges us to do, more by example than by direct exhortation, is — rather than centering on our particular sins, no matter how many and how great they may be, or how shameful, miserable, mean and little — to center on God's love. This will inevitably demand that we humble ourselves, confess, and repent as we realize how we fail in our response to it. At the same time it opens the way to our entering more and more fully into that way of love with all its potential for total divinization. It is the way of possibility and hope that can enkindle and respond to the idealism and enthusiasm of youth. This is far more healthy than centering upon our particular sins and thus upon ourselves, and ourselves as failures, which can lead us into our darker side and into depression and despair. Youth has enough to cope with without increasing any of this dark burden. Aloysius, despite the unfortunate popular images of him and some of the less happy images of him that have come down to us, is a saint of light. But a gentle, humble, quiet saint of light — one easy to befriend and to accept as a friend, to welcome into our lives. He makes no imperious demands, yet as we walk side by side with him he quietly challenges us to be the best we can be and always promises that more is possible. He is a friend who has the "guts" (read: the gift of fortitude, full out) to quietly do what is heroic as though it was the most natural thing in the world, the thing you would expect to do. If only the false imaging could be swept out of the way so that today's young men (and women, too, though I think of Aloysius as a man's man) could easily welcome him into their lives! We need friends like him.

The inner peace, the sureness, the serenity that prevailed in the life of Aloysius as he went about living his "ordinary" heroism, is something that attracts young people today. They would like to find that peace, to get in touch with the source of it.

Saint Mary Magdalene dei Pazzi had a vision of Aloysius only eight years after his death. I like the way she summed up the essence of his holiness: "kept his soul open to the interests of the Word. . . ."

He centered his interest, his love in another — the other being God, the creating and revealing Word who guides us and walks with us in the flesh of Jesus. When we can forget ourselves and open ourselves to living a love that centers in the interests and concerns of another, we do find peace and meaning in our lives. Even more so is this true when our love opens us to receive the love of that other and in our lover's eyes we begin to see something of our own beauty and wholeness. When that lover is God, then we can not only see the wholeness of our beauty but we can see our beauty and goodness constantly magnified and amplified in Their constantly creative love. We are directly in touch with the source of all peace and joy. To live "the interests of the Word" is the not-so-secret secret of Aloysius and the way he opened to the source of his deep serenity and quiet heroism.

Before we hold up Aloysius to our younger people as an exciting role model, perhaps we who are older and more responsible in the Catholic community need to examine what we are doing lest we inadvertently engender ever greater frustration. Idealism and enthusiasm still live in the hearts of the best of our youth, but where does it find an opportunity for expression in our institutional communities? Most parishes are wholly geared to married couples and children. Young men and women in high school are treated the same as children, and graduates are expected to go off to college and find their programs there. When they return and marry, they can become active participants in the parish. No wonder so many of our fine young Catholic men and women have found their place with Maharishi Mehesh Yogi, Mr. Moon, and the like. These masters tell them: You can make a difference, you can help change the world. And they give them the opportunity to begin to do that, to take leadership roles.

The idealism that engenders vocations still comes alive in hearts at sixteen, seventeen, eighteen. These young people will not be content with CYO sports and dances. They want and need something deeper. Where are the teachers and guides who will open up to these young the ways of the Spirit that so fed the young Aloysius? If Maharishi can spawn a meditation movement with young leadership, why cannot there be a Christian meditation movement where young meditators can initiate others and lead groups? And then go on to express their deeper sense of the whole Christ in social outreach.

Religious orders are rightly slow today to accept men or women at seventeen. Maturation seems a slower process now than in earlier times. Yet the idealism that hears the call still often comes quite early. The attempt to bridge the gap with college programs, while well-intentioned, is usually not very successful because it is not sufficient. What remains basically a college frat house with some pious exercises thrown in doesn't really respond to what is, perhaps unconsciously, sought. There needs to be the time and the space to receive a true formation in the Spirit and then to really give oneself to ministry and service, as did the young Aloysius. The scholastic should be fitted into the religious life rather than the religious squeezed into the scholastic. The meaning and need of the studies will become apparent — if they are really needed — and will be meaningfully undertaken in due time. The call is to a deeper life in the Spirit and to active expressions of that. Years of study imposed too soon can deaden that. Aloysius lived his life as a religious and died a saint before he completed his studies. If studies had pushed aside the deep spiritual growth he experienced in his late teen years and the ministry in which he expressed that self-giving spirit in his early twenties, he might have lived a long life as a religious, and we might not have a patron we like to propose as a model for our youth.

We do not do well as a faith community when we set forth for our young a model and then do not give them any really practical help or opportunity to live as that model lived. If we do not become a community more concerned about cultivating a deep life in the Spirit, whom we have all received at baptism, and more concerned about opening the space for our young people to give expression to their idealism and enthusiasm within our community, we will continue to lose our best and most gifted no matter what model we set up for them. Aloysius' example has perhaps more to say — and more immediately — to those in responsible leadership than to our youth.

Aloysius was a mystic in the same authentic sense in which each of us is called to be a mystic. He lived out the potential of his baptism. He let the indwelling Spirit form and lead him, and he courageously listened and followed, no matter what the cost. God did seem to be in a hurry with him. That corresponded to his intense nature: Grace builds on nature, the nature God gives us. For God, who dwells in eternity, time is not that important. God finishes the work of creation and recreation, if we allow Them, and then takes us to heaven. The things we do to slow down Their work in us only costs us in the end. Aloysius was willing and more than willing to pay the price from an early age. He made his mistakes. We make ours — perhaps quite different. These do not prevent God from getting on with the work. The exaggerations of Aloysius' impetuous nature should not put us off. Rather, they should encourage us, assuring us that the defects that come from our natural bent will not prevent God from bringing us to true holiness, to true mysticism, a life that is Spirit-led.

May Aloysius' very ordinary mysticism inspire us all and may his intercession help us all to become true mystics.[6]

NOTES

1. Herbert Thurston, S.J., has 395 pages of *The Physical Phenomena of Mysticism* (Chicago: Regnery, 1952).

2. Gabriel Diefenbach, *Common Mystical Prayer* (Paterson, N.J.: St. Anthony Guild Press, 1947).

3. E. I. Watkin, *The Bow in the Cloud* (New York: Macmillan, 1932), p. 165, quoted by Diefenbach, pp. 27-28.

4. Ibid.

5. I use plural pronouns and pronominal adjectives in referring to God to acknowledge that God is three divine persons.

6. There is no really good biography of Aloysius Gonzaga available. And maybe there cannot be one, for so much of the contemporary witness is couched in the excesses of the piety of the times that it is difficult to ferret out the truth of the matter. Meschler's, written for the third centenary and first published in 1911 but recently republished, is probably as good as any for containing the facts and a judicious selection of the writings: Maurice Meschler, S.J., *Saint Aloysius Gonzaga. Patron of Christian Youth* (Rockford, Ill.: TAN Books, 1985).

IX

Short and Sweet; and Against All Odds: A Life of Some Moment

Daniel J. Berrigan, S.J.

A kind of El Dorado of the spirit, rich, unlikely. And yet there it is, the story of a saint. A very lode of riches!

My image owes nothing to conventional piety; it is drawn from experience, specifically (and in my case with infinite good luck) from the experience of friendship.

This linkage of heart and hand with someone who stands close in one's life is, it seems to me, of the essence. The essence of what we call, too clumsily, our humanity. There is a fabulous concordance here; the nearness of one friend (not necessarily a saint) illumines the distant one, the saint. Because I have been blessed with friends for the space of a rather long life (one which promises on a daily basis to last even longer) I stretch out my hand to such as Aloysius, tentatively no doubt, even timorously. And I feel an answering warmth, a pressure and presence. And death shall have no dominion!

One who has known a friend will be forever impatient of others' versions of the friend. One simply knows. Others may or may not know. If my friend has died and someone sets to work writing an account of his life, I will scrutinize the writing with a kind of jealous, even picayune urgency. The thing must be gotten right! And if it is not right, but distorted, out of kilter, unjustly critical or carping; or on the other hand choked with pieties; if the image of my friend is cast, as it were, in dead plaster — then I am outraged, offended.

My friend was no saint, at least not according to your image of a saint!

Each of the above has happened to me; the distortion of a

friend's memory, the consequent outrage. One knows the friend, one is still a friend, though death intervened. Then one becomes the guardian of memory, even the guardian angel. This is the continuing office and honor of friendship. No betrayal of that office!

Sometimes the only form and dignity of the office, as the gravediggers sift the grave, is silence.

Aloysius has been badly dealt with. He deserved so much better of us who came after, especially of those who, centuries later, followed him into the Jesuits.

I have a sense also that larger questions are implied here. If we are to understand our vocation, to gain an inkling of the intention of Jesus with regard to Jesuits, we were well advised to grant more than a cursory salute in the direction of our saints.

There was a veritable cult of Jesuit saints urged on us from the day we entered the Order. Images of Jesuit saints, baroque imports and imitations all, populated (some would say pullulated) the chapel and grounds of the novitiate, a ghostly marmoreal assembly. (Indeed a priest remarked acidly one day that if, in reciting his breviary out of doors, he were to pause in his tracks, in a twinkling some novice or other was on his knees before him!)

A family sense was in the air. These brothers had walked the same track as ourselves, undergone the same regime of study and prayer and loneliness and camaraderie, had pronounced the same vows — had known the rigors and shoals of the common life, had seen their brows furrow and their pulse quake, what with exams, studies, years interminable.

This could be said as a matter of literal truth; our novitiate of fifty two years ago, but for such accidentals as electric lights and plumbing, in no substantial way differed from the Roman novitiate of Aloysius.

Talk about brothers, talk about friendship, that long black line was a very blur across the centuries! A million Jesuits have walked it, someone has estimated.

So I keep pondering Aloysius, the contrast, the covenant, the vow, the meaning. Even a phosphoric trace in the dark. All or any of these. The heart and longing and hope that arose in him from a small boy, a life of purpose, goodness, sweetness; and all so brief, crushed out of due season.

A sense of the true distance, perhaps — not the false, ephemeral, concocted, spectacular one — between his age and mine, his striving and love and terror, and mine. The necromancers and legenders have widened the gap until the saint is beyond attaining, a freak in nature. And what then of us mortals?

A way to bridge the distance.

Through the Gospel, how else?

What a contrast, his story and mine — or for that matter, his story and that of the great majority of Jesuits! We who for the most part sail into the order peaceably, with the blessing of parents and peers. We whose families are poor, working class, middle class.

And then the distance, as I would seek to understand it, not easily traversed. The nobility, the castle, cardinals and high officials of the realm for blood relations. Access to the great ones, ease and arrogance of gesture, servants and sycophants, pomp and circumstance at every turn, indulgence of every whim. And for his future, life-and-death power over the powerless.

All too easy to make of this youngster, fighting for his soul's ransom against enormous odds, an icon just short of bizarre, carefully and studiously remote, nose in air, rapt gaze, crucifix, lilies delicately in hand, cleaving his way to heaven with scant interest or attention to mere earthlings.

He was tougher than his would-be admirers would have him, both tougher and more tender, enormously more complex, his heaven won by way of many a detour — through hell.

One knows too that writing of Aloysius cannot be a matter of "objectively" setting down the facts. What is "objective" anyway? and what are these famous "facts," so often incanted? Can a fact concerning a human life stand by itself, uncolored by emotion, passion, relation, panic, high and low appetite?

To stay with the facts is to bury his corpse twice.

Poorly equipped as one is to approach Aloysius, one sets out nonetheless — on a rather horrific journey (even in this year, at this stage of my life) — the journey toward him, and that aura, enigma (distance again), puzzlement, the coloration and tone of his life, repelling and beckoning both. The excessive (so it would seem at first glance) self-disciplining, self-punishment even.

The heartbreaking effort called for, if he was to breathe free, to cut the noose so delicately woven, of money and prestige and lust and altitudinous pride of life. The tyranny of the bloodline (the world's offertory), the family's ambiguous tie.

And then the fraying of these bonds, by prayer and tears and bloodletting. His own blood. More than fraying, a clean cut of the lifeline.

The scandal, plainly put, offered by one so young, so singularly summoned, so eager to risk everything, so paying up. Cut the lifeline!

It was strangling him.

The harsh clarity of it, the single-minded intent and purpose, set against all claimants, intruders, controllers. A mother's tears, a father's fury. Opposition against such legitimate cries and whispers is so rare as to seem obsessive, even pathological. Except that the bloodshot purpose went hand in hand with a great sweetness, an affectionate heart that bled for the trouble it raised. Even as it insisted on its own beat.

He and ourselves. The distance. It is, as one freely admits, partly a cultural puzzle.

His age is one of noblesse oblige. The "first families" are proud, greedy, sumptuous in style, violent and valiant both, jealous of their perquisites, dead set against dispensing caviar to the general.

Their males, secular or ecclesiastical, are termagants. Of their women, predictably enough, little is heard or known.

I clap hands in the dark and whisper in half belief, "Miracle!"

A male of that line, "bloody, bold, and resolute," died of the consequences not of violence — of compassion.

For our sesquipedalian myths of "equality, fraternity, etc.," the Gonzagas would show only contempt; in their view the words are meaningless chatter, flying in the face of blood and breeding, paying tribute to a dubious version of the world and the human.

Their version rife with pride of place, ours with — leveling.

Let us not attempt to democratize Aloysius! No leveling this one; elegance to the fingertips, nobility of spirit, a relentless fiery courage, a choice to go it alone. Then the price he paid, declining the myth of the world as to its claim on such as he. Breaking the mythological clutch (a family affair as well).

The price of all this. (The price we [I] renege on).

As though great things can be cheaply won; and not turn paltry in the winning.

And yet, and yet. When it is exacted today, this debt of honor, it is paid, all said, in no other coin than his. (When it is paid.) Indeed one cannot easily demonstrate that the "*itinerarium Deo*," in his era or our own, has become a cheap trip.

Or that the coin laid in the palm of Christ, face up, has ever borne another face than — Caesar's.

There is no coin of the realm that dares show the face of Christ.

Mammon. The face on the coin and the metal of the coin are one.

The face is devouring; it is a face forged on an anvil of war and plunged in the fires of injustice. Thus the prophets, who traded in another coinage. Thus Christ.

A confident face, above all. It lays its bets — on itself. Hail Caesar, hail silver and gold! This is the cry of the coin, the cry the world takes up in a great chorus, the claim laid on the life of the one who palms the coin, lusts after, keeps, trades in it.

But in the instance of Christ, something else; a cool-handed letting go. Render unto whom you will. But not in My name!

How this "render unto Caesar" (the words were surely pronounced in the first incident with an all but ineffable irony) — how this was understood by Aloysius — in his follow-through, his vocation, the choice that brought him to an early death, the kiss imprinted on the leper — the events themselves may be thought to illustrate.

To wit; nothing for Caesar.

This could only strike fire.

In the mind of those who called the tune, including his own family, the "unto Caesar" was something else; a large tribute indeed, presupposed, touted up, handed over in installments. It was simply the common debit and patrimony.

One could, with small embarrassment and deft handling and a bargain struck with Church and State, render unto God and make substantial payment to Caesar as well.

Again and again, the debt come due; a common understanding, a nod, a concession. The tune they all danced to. All went well in the castles, to the great advantage of all. (Or nearly all.)

129

All was likewise secure, dank, and silent in the castle keep. There is a dark side of great fortunes.

A male infant, baptized amid the ancestral lace and linen, was to the manor born. (Also to the keep born, and the bridge of sighs, and the unspeakable that lay behind the splendid salons.)

Thus it was decreed at his birth; Aloysius would benefit from the inheritance, would exert himself in view of its prospering, would pass on the increment. This was beyond argument, a law of nature, a decree from on high; it bound the newborn like a swaddling band. Birthright implied birth duty.

Noblesse oblige! The social fabric was as closely drawn as a stellar map. Dante had said as much, mapping the universe from hell to heaven. Thomas Aquinas had expounded the natural law, "governing all rational beings."

Indeed the stars of heaven in their courses, as Jesuits were reminded by their founder, served as form and fabric of sensible earthly arrangements, including those of Church, State, and the new Order.

The arrangements were not only governed by an unarguable "natural" law. This is the lesser story. Hierarchy, lowerarchy, command, obey, these were — godly. They bespoke the divine will, were to be venerated and obeyed as such.

That the same arrangements had an aura of the macho-hierarchico, that a higher "arche" implied a lower, a winner a loser — of what concern could this be to a mere child? The pavanne of the universe, as reflected in courtly life, went on. It drowned out with a heartless, careless blare the cries from the castle keep, the torture, the misery of a landless peasantry, the ceaseless wars.

As to the manner or timing of their death, the dead had no vote.

How then to respond, to beggars at the door, to misery abroad? The response, where it occurred at all, was one of largesse, charity.

And what of justice?

The question did not occur. This world, the real one, ours *in saecula saeculorum*. A closed system, self-sufficient, self-justified.

Could the God of such a culture be thought to dwell anywhere but amid the splendors, ease, privilege?

To dwell, let us say, in the servants' corner of existence, among the peasantry, the captives, in the squalid back streets of villages, the seamy underside of existence?

The question did not commonly arise.

The crucifixes were wrought of ivory and silver.

It is a lost cause Aloysius moves toward, embraces like a lover, and with inexorable haste dies for. Let it be admitted, freely, bitterly, as case may be. Admitted, the evidence, the lost cause. The centuries that follow serve only to multiply the evidence, even as they multiply the corpses, the victims, the misery, the unspeakable hardening of heart afflicting the powerful.

To wit: The cause of Aloysius, which he made his own, as though an incandescent glance had passed between himself and Christ, as though at that glance a shudder shook his being, as though he dwelt thereafter in a stupendous end time of signs and wonders, as though he was stigmatized (in more senses than one) — his cause is a perennial lost cause. It is wearisome, discredited, clumsy, foolish, in the eyes of the world.

Were it not for the fame and family of Aloysius (and the fame and family of the One who beckoned) — the cause would be largely undocumented, a matter of fools and freaks and malcontents. How often we have heard it! The cause is "reminiscent," in a contemptuous sort of way (so the world-weary judgment goes, with a yawn, a superior smile) of whatever former generation (of lost causes).

Aloysius and his ilk! despite all, they undertake the cause anew — adding so it is said, another dolorous chapter to the log of the centuries; lost, lost.

The announcement of the "loss" of the cause is of course made by the principalities of this world, whose cause, in the nature of things, must be understood everywhere and always as winning, prevailing, crushing, invading, lying, murdering.

And in the process of winning, guaranteeing also, with fire and sword, contempt and ostracism, the law's rigor (the castle keep) — that the Lords of Loss lose again.

And shrugging it all off; no accountability.

To speak of the world of Aloysius is, willy-nilly, to speak of his family. This family forbade his longings, sought to tighten its grip. His father at his throat; fury, rhetoric, tears. Did he not owe them etcetera? Was he not the scion of a long and noble etcetera?

Hence a law of physics must be invoked; for every coil a spectacular recoil.

One might think (it has often been thought), How excessive the recoil of this child!

(Our own response to worldly enticement being something else; in a word coined since his time, a matter not greatly superior to — sleaze.)

Ideal families. Ideal families as Christian families. This is a notable fiction, purveyed in the time of Aloysius and our own time.

His family comes onstage as "ideal." They formed a social clot that worked ideally, to their benefit, for a long time.

Something about them commonly escapes notice. A disturbing resemblance, in spite of that persistent "Christian" tag. A species of elegant greed, a love of this world. Like every pagan family of their land (or of any land), they levied onerous taxes, collected same to the last penny, kept close accounts, guarded their property and investments, held their male progeny closely accountable to the future of same, intermarried among their own, weighed loss and gain in advance of such unions.

To Aloysius, the style, the interlocking directorate, the vanity and folly, the emptiness were a horror.

One might have thought, What a favored existence! Life is pelting him with roses! In fact, he was wounded and thwarted.

The family, in the way of great clans, wanted above all to tame him. Loyalty, esprit, the escutcheon, the estates, the bloodline. These were the imperatives. They governed life and intentions and behavior, they lent a superior patina and form to an otherwise ambiguous and violent age.

And in any case, what were the alternatives, why indeed seek alternatives, when one had been born into a world whose form was a tipped cornucopia?

Ideal families? We who survive such purported wonders, or perpetuate them, had best grow reflective. Christ was embarrassingly skeptical on the matter; he turned a cold eye on his own family, it would seem. (And they on him!)

The "ideal Christian family" of Aloysius, as matters developed, became a formidable obstacle to his following of Christ. The story is not to be thought exceptional. Very few "Christian families" so comport themselves — with regard to such worldly realities as money, sex, authority — as to serve as seedbeds for a rigorous lifelong vow.

Long years ago, we too were Jesuit novices on our way to glory.

One of the presiding fictions of that place and time, told of the ideal Christian (read Catholic) family. Out of this genetic wonder had sprung, as though by a natural fusion of controlled delights, the holy sprout who presently was prepared to enhance the Order.

It was all nonsense. Nonsense nonetheless firmly clung to. A scene comes to mind.

In the visiting parlor, where the novices were allowed a few hours' respite with "externs" every few months, a kind of prelapsarian satisfaction prevailed. The Jesuit Fathers and parents alike rejoiced genteelly in a common beatitude: Blessed be the parents, blessed be the unblemished offspring.

The facts were otherwise. We were one and all, or nearly all, case examined, sprung from families who labored under the onerous burden of the culture. Catholicism might be our virtuous front; but it resolved little or nothing of the violence of our world; alcoholism, abuse of women, McCarthyism, racism, the world at war, the whole lot.

(Is it allowed at this point to confess, I hold Aloysius dear, I wish I had known him, I think we could have been friends? At least I hope such is the case. I sense the nobility, the poise, the delicate balance, the "beauty and valor and act." And the tears exacted, if against such odds, he was to reach the finish.

(I hope he would have liked me, approved [with reservations and arguments allowed, indeed incumbent on friends, and greatly beneficial too] the way I have gone.

(May we someday meet, and sit down to such matters. Indeed we will.)

He illustrates in his brief sojourn another vexed matter, that of the insider and the outsider. That the world should be so arranged, that many must suffer so that a few may rejoice — he came to understand

the situation as sinful, criminal. It was his first experience of —
plague.

He cast off the infection.

It came about gradually, the strengthening of his immunity. The
Gospel was, so to speak, strong medicine.

Those few who were born insiders, or who in victorian imagery
were granted "Great Expectations," had only the vaguest idea of the
sea of misery that surrounded them. Vague idea, small concern. They
sailed in a grand galleon, a veritable ship of fools. No idea of the
misery which their own affluence and pride of place created.

Theirs was, as the poet said, a painted ship upon a painted ocean.
Was this not heaven's decree? Did not the priests assure them that a
favorable passage through life was their plain due, an irrefutable
evidence of divine favor?

Then the vast majority of the shipwrecked, then as now, the aliens,
the "undocumented," those outside the pale.

And *eccolo*! the Aloysius breed. Changelings, insiders cursed or
blessed with an eye capable of a closer and a wider view.

Did the Jesuits see themselves as Aloysius saw them, and was
drawn to them — a vowed coterie of outsiders? outside the norm, the
dead center, the institutional mammon, collusion with the high and
mighty? Certainly the *Spiritual Exercises* of Ignatius speak
unequivocally. Jesuits are to follow Christ in His shameful passion, to
accept tranquilly the slings and arrows of the world. Or so it is written.

Still, from the beginning, indeed in Aloysius' lifetime, an irony,
a contradiction arose. The wealthy and noble were sedulously
cultivated (as they are today). The story of Aloysius moves along in
a kind of Bayeux tapestry of light and ambiguity. In the
communities, hair-raising personal austerities were simply the
norm. No one owned anything, nor, as far as can be judged, longed
to do so. They set out on mission, across Europe, across the world,
with "neither scrip nor staff."

But money, money became a large matter; there were colleges to
be built and endowed and maintained. Thus the rub.

One can be pardoned for speculating. According to reports,
Aloysius was held in unusual honor during his short life in the
Society. It was perhaps inevitable; his noble birth, spectacular

renunciation, self-effacing piety, all conspired to make of him a legend larger than life.

But suppose he survived into old age with ideals intact, would the legend also have survived? Or would he be shunted aside, barely tolerated in a coterie of classic — insiders?

He stepped over a line, he went with a terrible deliberateness, beyond the pale. The act was altogether gratuitous; it was a lightning bolt, it was grace, too close; God speaking, God hearkened to. And this by one who had ample reason to ignore or explain away the summons.

No more logic drove him along the way he went. No cardinal or pope or parent or peer, good Christians all according to the canons of that time (or this), spoke for him, offered support. Quite the opposite.

It was grace. And we are afraid.

There is something very old in this, a tradition never quite broken, even by the keepers of the tradition. The best they can do (and it is often the worst) is to "guard" the tradition.

This is the office they hold, or seize upon. It is hostile toward such as Aloysius. To be sure, they do not guard the tradition against the onslaught of such as themselves; they guard it often as not against the saints. In whom they sense a furious resistance, as the decapitated head, rattling its vain moralisms, declares itself the sum total of the body of Christ.

Against such, Aloysius understood, there was no argument. He has nothing to say to this argument. He was in the world to offer another argument entirely.

His was the argument of the inarticulate, the inchoate, the unborn. The death-row inmate. The non-citizen. Of those who have no stake in the world. Of those who in fact clutter the nation state, impede its rogue's progress, and depart this world to a sussuration of relief. Who are born unwanted or prove themselves of no use. Worse, who care to prove nothing, produce nothing.

Whose demise in consequence, is accounted a good riddance, since they are neither purse-proud nor property grabbers nor good consumers. Nor will they march in lock step or kill on command.

The vocation of Aloysius, be it admitted, in no wise slowed, let alone derailed, the world's humming engine.

135

Pitifully short, and hardly sweet, history. A youth donned a Jesuit cassock. Shortly thereafter, with the blessing of his superiors, he began to succor a few anonymous plague victims. Then he died — of the plague. The least one can say (and perhaps the most), and in muted celebration, is that the Noble Youth Who Died Young opened a way for many others.

Living the Gospel, he verified the Gospel anew. That book, that book!

It was tossed about, abused, closed, opened, slammed shut again in the world's wild winds. The text was hidden away in Irish towers (actually) and in Dead Sea caves. Time did its worst, and barbarians, and "experts."

The text was all but obliterated.

Or something else occurred; the eyes of the beholder were blinded. Then the text was amended and explained away, modified, softened or made rigid in the hands of abusive scribes.

Who was to reclaim the word of God, hold it steady, con it with intensity and tears, swear a great vow as to its living truth?

A brief, intense flare went up in the night. Many saw and took heart. A few texts sufficed; he held them by heart. "Come follow me," "Take up your cross." Christ, His life and death and rising. He underwent the mysteries; then He went under.

Dante comes to mind, the "*punto*" of the *Inferno*, the "rose" of the *Paradiso*. The "center" was more than a "medieval world view," more than a "modern" or a "preChristian"; it was simply Christ's world view. On that point, the Gospel was embarrassingly clear.

This center would radiate outward (as it did in Dante's time and in preceding and following centuries). Its circumference would include time and culture and history and future and family and individual lives; of course. Every life, every institution, every eon, all were included, embraced.

And the misery too, the mystery of those "at the edge," barely hanging on, falling off. The plague-stricken of every age, the "marginalized," the AIDS children, the innocents of Iraq, the Kurds. Into death they go, after a fate that seems at once bizarre in chanciness and banal in outcome.

But the center must hold firm. Despite all, Christ at center. Not a static article of faith or an ideology or "world view." A stark and only hope. Without it the circumference dissolved in a void.

Did his eye rest on the Center, or on those languishing at the edge? On both. Simultaneously.

So young, so untried in the world by reason of wealth and nobility, Aloysius sought the center.

And then the Jesuits, and a sea change; he found himself pushed to the edge, the terror of the shadowy circumference, the void.

It was a taste of death; at first, of the death of others, as he tried by whatever slim means available, to assuage the onslaughts of the plague. And then — something else; his own illness, his death at hand, young as he was, and everything in his favor. All unexpected, that brutal outcome.

"A child of his times," so some have dismissed him (the self-lacerated body, the fasts, the pernickety distancing from family and "inordinate affection," the relentless self-scrutiny, the firm stand at the side of the underdog).

"A child of his times"; one senses a half-indulgent nod in the direction of the follies and foibles of his century (and of himself by implication). After all, after all, small matters. Matters which, by a prestidigitation of sorts, become then strengths of our own time.

Superior to all that! by reason of psychology and technology and mass communication and mass murder, by temperance and prudence and the "via aurea," by just-war theory and slave camps and smart bombs, by a first-world church waving a minatory finger at the martyr church of the third world.

By these , it would seem, we put on display our genius in grasping at — nonessentials.

For fear of the essential, the dire implications of the "come follow me"?

Aloysius grasped at the essential. It was thorny, and his body bled for it.

As for taming him, the Jesuits knew better than to try. They gave him both spur and scope, and he raced for the finish.

When the distinguished novice walked through their Roman portal, the Jesuits were a young order of only forty-five years. It was a good match. He was joining a community whose history was yet to be written; indeed his life and death were to form a glorious chapter of that history.

Now under strict guidance, his fervent soul would mature. He would be obedient to the least jot and tittle, would fast and wear his body with watching and chains and disciplines, and never be alone on the arduous journey — as in his family he had been so long alone.

"*Erant in illis diebus gigantes.*" In those early days, giants walked the earth.

He could also in due time risk his life, and be blessed for it. What was life for, except to risk, to be given away? The prospering of institutions had yet to assume a large importance. Jesuits lived with kind of lighthearted careless care; in the breach, in the moment, one thinks buddhistically.

Not only creature comforts were spurned; "earthly life" itself was held in no high regard. Heaven was a siren call in the soul. They had taken the name of Jesus as the name of their order; so they walked to the beat of that heart.

"The things which are unseen!" The present world, its emoluments and favors, were dismissed with a Pauline scorn; "*stercorea.*"

There were the older orders, venerable to be sure; they were planted in the Church centuries before, they moved majestically, assured of perpetuity; Benedictines, Franciscans, Dominicans.

But there was nothing in Church or world quite like this; the forwardness and cheek, the vitality, the world-encompassing vision, the outright chutzpah of those first-generation Jesuits. For good and ill, they would mount the Counter-Reformation throughout Europe, would send their noblest members across the world on errands that could only be termed quixotic. (That old canard — lost causes. They were very entrepreneurs of lost causes.)

And at home they landed this great catch, the patrician Luigi. It was remarkable how skillfully they played the line, how they won father and son alike. The father somewhat dissolute and more than somewhat stiff-necked, raging and vowing and forbidding from his gouty sickbed: No son of mine! etc.

And yet, shortly after the son's departure, the father made peace with the recusant, and shortly thereafter a good death.

The newly arrived, fervent, highly developed spirit was allowed his awesome scope.

In time, all things in good time.

Did he seek to serve the plague-stricken? Let him do so, at risk of life.

Let him in the effort lose his life.

It could only be accounted a good ending, befitting.

The prize, the prize!

And death no dominion.

X

A Friend on the Journey

Martin F. Blair

My grandfather, Samuel Aloysius Halliday, immigrated to the United States in the winter of 1899. A native of a mill town in Northwest England, Grandaddy had grown weary of the discrimination frequently inflicted upon Roman Catholics in the Victorian "Rule Britannia" era of British history. He was also from an extraordinarily poor family. However, Grandaddy was educated by the Jesuits, and he remained devoted to the Society of Jesus for the rest of his life. Through his teachers, he was introduced to Saint Aloysius Gonzaga, a dominant figure in the Catholic Church of his childhood. On the deck of a dilapidated (and barely seaworthy) ship that crossed the Atlantic Ocean that winter, Grandaddy clutched a holy card bearing the image of Gonzaga and believed that the Jesuit "Boy Saint" traveled alongside him.

To my grandfather, Aloysius Gonzaga represented everything that was truly Christian and authentically Catholic. He was a Renaissance prince who had rejected power, wealth, and prestige to serve the poor as a Jesuit. Much like the first followers of Ignatius Loyola, Gonzaga was not frightened when such service involved nursing victims of the plague. It was a choice which ultimately resulted in his death at the age of twenty-three.

Grandaddy often compared Aloysius to Francis of Assisi: the two men were Italian aristocrats, hailing from families of influence and privilege. Most importantly, they had embraced the message of the Gospel with utter simplicity and generosity.

Years later, his grandchildren would roll their eyes and flee the room when he told stories about Aloysius. I remember thinking that they were sentimental but brought out a tenderness in the man that we rarely saw. I can also remember a cousin imitating the statue of

Gonzaga which Grandaddy kept in his bedroom; his eyes dramatically lifted to the ceiling, a crucifix clutched to his chest, a mock altar-boy robe draped across his shoulders. My cousin entered the room and began to lecture the rest of us.

"I'm Grandaddy's best friend," he proclaimed. "My name is Aloysius and I'm PURE!"

We roared in approval that day, but I never forgot the stories about Grandaddy's "friend." Eventually, I realized that the "Patron Saint of Purity" was never a part of those anecdotes. Perhaps, I reasoned, there were two Gonzagas: the plaster-cast saint with the strange white complexion and a blank, beatific stare; and the trusted friend who held my Grandfather's hand as he set off to find a better life in America.

Aloysius, the boy virgin, was a fragment of a human being, a one-dimensional caricature of chastity under ice.

The Gonzaga of my childhood was flesh and blood. He was a social activist. He was a prince. He was powerfully close to God.

Years later, when I was studying for the priesthood as a Jesuit, I encountered the same duality. During a homily, a priest told us that Gonzaga epitomized "the chastity of the angels," but his description of the saint's life had all the warmth of a stained-glass window. Once again, I wondered whether people knew that there had been more to Aloysius than his much-celebrated chastity.

During my seminary years, a fellow scholastic attended a Halloween party as the saint, winning accolades for a costume remarkably similar to the outfit modeled by my cousin. He also drew laughter for a devastating imitation of Gonzaga's "Modesty of the Eyes": the scholastic banged into walls, collided with furniture, slammed people with an oversized crucifix, and seemed nervously incapable of any form of human interaction.

A historical review easily disputes this cliché of Gonzaga's life: according to existing records, Aloysius was respected for his intelligence, his personal warmth, and his humility. He would have been deeply embarrassed that the habit of lowering his eyes in public (probably a survival skill acquired during his years at court) would be urged upon other religious as a sign of virtue. Aloysius wanted to disappear in the "long black line" of the Society and shunned anything that would single him out from his fellow Jesuits.

This is not to suggest that Aloysius was anything less than superbly acquainted with what we now describe as the art of public relations. After all, he spent his childhood in one of the most decadent royal courts of European history. Named in honor of a founding member of the Gonzaga dynasty that ruled Mantua for centuries, Aloysius was destined to continue the family line and succeed his father. Carefully biding his time and navigating the power struggles of his clan (which included several prominent Church leaders), he entered the Jesuits with the blessing of his family, an astonishing triumph of faith, determination, and astute public relations.

It is my view that the Church eventually made Aloysius a victim of the very prayers he inspired. How could a handsome, vigorous historical figure survive a proclamation as the "Patron Saint of Catholic Youth," becoming a symbol of the Church's inherently negative views on human sexuality? While the Catholic Church battled to press its political influence, Gonzaga's cult was a viable weapon against the newly empowered rulers and nationalistic leaders. Here was a young prince who had chosen to sacrifice his life for the Church: in other words, how dare you challenge the Supreme Pontiff of Rome when such a remarkable saint marches under his banner?

Therefore, the currents of history and cultural views on sexuality conspired against Aloysius Gonzaga. As the Church struggled to renew itself in modern times, Aloysius was left behind. A Jesuit I knew went as far as to suggest that the canon of Jesuit saints needed some "weeding out" of individuals "unsuitable for our times." At the top of his list was Aloysius Gonzaga.

However, in the words of my grandfather, "Nothing changes faster in life than change itself."

He would be pleased to see the changes that are taking place right now concerning his beloved saint.

In particular, thousands of men and women who are victims of today's modern plague, AIDS, are finding comfort and courage in the witness of Gonzaga's life. They do not see the otherworldly saint with the uplifted eyes, walking several inches in the air, blissfully removed from the challenges of life: they see a young man who voluntarily entered the darkness of disease, discrimination, and poverty, lighting a flame that has never been extinguished. They see a real historical

142

figure who embraced the outcasts of his time, who carried their bodies and nursed their wounds at risk to his own health. They see a young man cut down in the prime of life who did not go gently into the night but left a legacy of love that transforms their lives.

Although the forms of devotion have changed, Grandaddy would have noted that the same people whom Aloysius served during his lifetime have once again sought his help.

Before he passed away in 1976, my grandfather predicted that I would leave the Jesuits before ordination.

The year before, I had visited the Church of the Annunciation in Florence and knelt at the spot where the young Aloysius had pledged to give his life to God. Grandaddy was pleased by my trip and wept when I described what I had seen; he was proud when I became a Jesuit novice in the fall of 1975.

But he openly questioned whether a rebellious individual such as myself was suited for community life. At the same time, I understood that the love and respect we shared would never change.

After seven years, I left the Jesuits and began a new career in broadcasting. With few links to either the Jesuits or the Church, I felt a growing chasm between the challenges of my life and the religious beliefs of my childhood.

But five years ago, something happened which brought Aloysius Gonzaga back into my life.

On Christmas Eve, I sat alongside the bed of a close friend who was dying from AIDS. During the night, a storm pounded rain against the hospital windows and thunder crashed above us. When my friend stirred awake, he looked up to see a group of his friends and family clustered around him, clothed and masked in yellow paper robes. The protective clothing was a requirement by the hospital, but my friend was startled and cried out in fear.

We stood there, paralyzed for a moment, and then pulled off the masks and robes, leaning forward to touch and reassure him.

Later, as I waited in the hall for the elevator, I was surrounded by a group of doctors, nurses, and hospital staff. When the elevator door opened, I quickly walked inside but no one joined me. I then heard complaints from the group, referring to the removal of the protective clothing in my friend's room. With the chorus of a

Christmas carol playing in the background, I also heard somebody describe me as "that faggot's friend," moments before the door shut between us.

Overcome with rage and grief, I had difficulty falling asleep that evening. When I finally rested, I had a dream unlike any I had ever had before.

In my dream, I stood inside that hospital elevator and listened once again to the comments from the group. I studied their faces and saw hatred, ignorance, and fear. Cold sweat broke out all over my body, and I suddenly felt as if I was about to be attacked. Thankfully, the door closed and I felt safe.

But a few seconds later, it opened on another floor, and a young man who I instantly recognized stepped in to join me.

It was Aloysius Gonzaga. He didn't say a word to me in my dream but placed one arm across my shoulder and gently embraced me, holding me until the elevator opened on the ground floor of the hospital.

Later, I realized that Aloysius, indeed, had spoken to me.

It was a simple message: "I understand."

Recently, I followed the example of my grandfather and told the story of Aloysius Gonzaga to my nine-year-old niece. She couldn't believe that a prince would renounce a throne to join the Jesuits. She was also astonished that Aloysius would walk the streets of Rome to seek out the homeless and the forgotten of his time.

"What was he trying to say?" she asked.

"He was trying to tell people that he loved them," I replied. Then, recalling the incident at the hospital and the dream that followed, I told her that Aloysius also wanted people to know that he "understood."

This is the message that I believe Aloysius Gonzaga wants to bring to our modern world. We may be fragmented by the demands made upon us, exhausted by a violent and increasingly desperate world, or troubled by the failure of our dreams and ideals. But Aloysius looks us squarely in the eyes and offers hope and comfort:

"I understand."

Louis M. Swift (taken by AIDS in 1990) before Guercino painting in the Metropolitan Museum

"St. Aloysius Gonzaga" by Guercino (1591-1666), Metropolitan Museum of Art, New York

St. Aloysius retablo (panel painting) by Charles Carrillo of Santa Fe, New Mexico

XI

Aloysius: A Reluctant Admiration

Ethel Pochocki

I began research for this essay with some reluctance, little admiration, and many questions. Who was this saint *really*? Why, after four hundred years, should he still be relevant? Why on earth, or in Heaven, would I want to know him, much less understand him? *What is he to me*?

Aloysius Gonzaga! His very name conjures up a scene of murky Renaissance intrigues and a time rife with murder and violence and familial warfare. (On that point, he might be quite relevant today.)

I admit that my reluctance may have had its roots in remembrances of holy cards past, those hoped-for prods to sanctity distributed by the nuns as bookmarks that life was short, death inevitable, the world was evil, so be on guard! The martyrs and Patrons of Youth were favorite subjects — Agnes, Lucy, the Holy Innocents, Maria Goretti, and, of course, Aloysius.

His picture was unappealingly otherworldly, a fragile boy in clerical garb, aristocratic face, pale skin, unsmiling, burning eyes, hair carefully slicked back (why, I wonder, were there never curly-headed saints with mischievous grins?), slender hands holding the essential lily. I was not drawn to him in the least. Now he would have his comeuppance. Now, in writing this essay, we would meet head on.

How does one begin to get beyond a mere shrugging tolerance of those with whom we feel we have nothing in common? My first step is to pull out my steady, sturdy, never-fail, always-on-tap, worn-thin-but-not-out belief in the Mystical Body. Here is where we all live; this is our Homeland, where we are welcome, secure, comfortable, equal but different in our unique gifts. Each of us is in our place at a particular time for a particular purpose, and only God knows why. Some lives will always remain an unknown liaison between soul and Creator, an irritating puzzle to those who live by theory and reason and need precisely fitting pieces. Human reason may not be satisfied with "Life is a mystery," but what else can be said of the unanswerable? Pontifical ponderings and psychological probing reflect only other human viewpoints; I find "life is a mystery" more satisfying.

This Mystical Body groans with an infinite variety of sanctity, for there is no entrance requirement but that saints and would-be saints love God and do his will, and if they aren't sure of His will, just do their honest best. That simple request allows all kinds in — butchers, beggars, lawyers, thieves, you, me. And how wonderfully encouraging that we have each other to lean on, to love, emulate, grab hold of in sudden need!

Saints have been our support groups long before we officially labeled such things. We had a list of certified heavenly helpers: Joseph, Anthony, Lucy, Francis de Sales, etc., each of whom specialized (rotten husband, bad eyes, lost keys, bar exam; Martin de Porres would even rid your attic of mice).

Beyond these wonderful household saints, there were the Others. We should not pigeonhole them into stereotypes, but they can be loosely categorized — the singles, the marrieds, the royals, the peasants, the social activists, the hermits, the crabs and cranks, and the young ones. Aloysius was one of these holy-from-birth saints, those intense, passionate, driven, single-minded ones, rushing pell-mell into holiness, steamrolling anyone in the way in their hurry to get back to God. They flash across the sky of our mundane lives so we might look up and gasp with wonder. They blazed briefly — Joan of Arc, Thérèse, Rose of Lima, Aloysius — God's sparklers, like Edna St. Vincent Millay's candle burning at both ends, which "will not last the night / But ah, my foes, and oh, my friends — / It gives a lovely light!"

So what did Aloysius do with his lovely light? From surface facts, he did not contribute to world peace or environmental causes. He did nothing to save the dolphins or the Lombardy poplar or promote democratic government. Aloysius' mission was in being rather than doing, and in following God's will. For him, this meant becoming a Jesuit against all odds.

Biographers give a skeleton of vital facts about his life which we must flesh out with our imagination and intuition, so that he does not remain a composite of hagiographers' opinions, or, as one writer put it, he does not come across as "a singularly pointless prig, a washed-out namby-pamby."

He was born in 1568 to Don Ferrante and Donna Marta Gonzaga, a royal family of Castiglione in the northern province of Lombardy. For three hundred years the Gonzagas had been fighting with other clans to obtain dominance in the area. He was born into a dark chaotic time, in which peace was the exception among the warring families.

Aloysius was earmarked for the army. At the age of five, he was brought by his father to a military camp where he shared the life of the soldiers and quickly became their doted-upon mascot. He marched with the men, took part in their drills, and picked up some of their colorful language. According to his biographers, when rebuked by his tutor for this, he was overcome with a remorse that never left him. In later years, he called this time his "period of sin."

At the age of seven, he had a "religious quickening." He began what would become his lifelong penitential practices, kneeling night and morning to pray on the stone floor. So complete was his surrender to God that, in the opinion of Robert Bellarmine, his confessor, Aloysius never committed a mortal sin.

When he was nine, he and his brother were sent to the court at Florence to learn Latin. The court life here was at best frivolous and foolish; at worst, unashamedly depraved and lustful. He was thrust face to face with a world he knew as dangerous to his soul. He made a vow of celibacy — already he was a known matrimonial catch, and the ladies of the court made no bones about making advances — and with his Northern Italian temperament of steely mind and passionate fervor, he vowed never to touch a woman or to look upon her. Even if he made polite conversation, he would not look her in the eye. When he was a Jesuit, he would not be alone in a room with a woman. Aloysius never did things by halves.

When he was eleven, his father moved the two boys to the court of the Duke of Mantua. A bout of kidney disease gave Aloysius a legitimate excuse to remove himself from court life, and he spent the time praying and reading books about the saints. A book about Jesuit missionaries in India planted the seed for his future as a Jesuit. He began zealous preparation. He fasted three days a week on bread and water, scourged himself regularly with a whip, and as before, knelt on the stone floor to pray.

When he approached his parents with his decision, his mother, with whom he was close, was pleased; his father was furious. If his son would not be a soldier, he fumed, then at least he must aspire to diplomat or statesman. Father and son, equally stubborn, were in conflict for years. Don Ferrante used every means of persuasion, cajoling or threatening, to rid his son of his foolishness. But Aloysius, immovable in his belief that God willed him to join the Jesuits, would not give in and finally won. At the age of eighteen, he became a Jesuit novice. Six weeks later, his father died.

Aloysius, finally freed of conflict, exulted in his new life and a new contentment. Despite his failing health, he asked for the most menial work, first in the kitchen, then, when the plague broke out in Rome, in the hospital the Jesuits opened. For one who could not stand the sight of blood or the stench of infection, this was a test of physical fortitude. Yet he returned each day, picking up the soiled dressings "with a little pounce" — we can imagine him steeling himself — and then cleaning and freshly dressing the wounds. When he was not in the hospital, he was on the streets, picking up fallen victims and carrying them on his back to the hospital. It was in this way he inevitably caught the fever and died on the Feast of Corpus Christi at the age of twenty-three.

A brief life. On the surface it might seem a familiar story of a headstrong, self-centered child determined to have his own way, despite the effect on his parents and country. He could have remained a prince, some argue, ruling his country as Ideal Despot, as other royal saints have done. But this was not Aloysius' way.

In Margaret Munro's perceptive book *A Book of Unlikely Saints* (Longmans Green, 1946), she writes about the conflict with his father and his giving up his ruling privileges:

> It is said that Aloysius took the easier path, preferring a "fugitive and cloistered virtue" to the courageous course, which was to live the Christian life in the world, leavening its evil with the force of his

example. . . . Aloysius had the power to give the people of Castiglione more equitable taxation, since heavy taxes were the curse of Italy and one cause of its frequent famines. . . . He threw up a responsible position in which he had immense opportunities of doing good, which he was called to by public opinion as well as by birth and his exceptional talents. And yet, with all this against him, Aloysius did convince us of the rightness of his choice. He did so by appealing to a principle our society no longer admits — a direct personal call from God. . . . Such a call welling up in the deeps of the individual, had to have utterly overwhelming urgency if it was to hold its own against the resistances encountered . . . which came not only from what wrong in the age, but even more poignantly from what it had of good and right.

How could it be God's will for Aloysius to give so much pain, to swerve from so great an opportunity of public service, to set his own soul before his fellowmen? . . . We cannot query Aloysius without also querying Christ. . . . We are so made that the teaching of Christ is apt to remain for us mere words, possibly even pretty-pretty words, until we see it embodied in a human life. . . . It is the Saints who hold before our eyes the Gospel embodied in contemporary life. Some saints belong wholly to their own epoch. In others, their revolutionary significance continues for generation, even centuries. Aloysius can do our age one great service — he can spur us to reconsider our picture of Jesus. . . . He will cleanse our minds from that unreal Jesus who is an amiable moralist interested in making the world safe for democracy. The real Jesus was not interested in making the world safe for anybody and His best exponents are those who live dangerously. . . .

"No one," she concludes, "was ever less likely material for grace than Aloysius Gonzaga, and few have had so complex a tangle to unravel."

Aloysius lived dangerously by responding to his unlikely, inexplicably bestowed, grace in a manner as unique as he was. He yearned for nothing but withdrawal from this world. For those of us who enjoy our transient stay on earth and its myriad comforts and blessings — strong coffee, old books, *Cheers*, chamber music, Dave

Barry — his penitential path may seem a harsh and alien one. But it was *his* path.

The rest of us in the Mystical Body might pray that we surrender as wholeheartedly to whatever unlikely grace comes our way. We are *all* unlikely material, but God is such an extravagant dispenser. Like picnickers caught without umbrellas in a summer squall, we never know when we will be drenched in an outpour. May we all revel in it as dangerously as Aloysius!

XII

Las Fiestas de San Luis Gonzaga en La Plaza de Nuestra Señora de Guadalupe de Los Griegos Albuquerque, Nuevo México

Andrés J. Segura

A t sunset on the twenty-first day of June each year, as it has been done for over a hundred years, a group of neighbors emerge from an old adobe home and begin a candlelight procession down an old road formerly known as the *Camino Real* with the statue of San Luis Gonzaga. He is carried by the people in rotation for the short journey, and the rosary is sung as the procession slowly moves along through the warm New Mexico summer evening.

The exact year that the celebration of the feast day in honor of San Luis Gonzaga began in Los Griegos is not known. Why this saint was chosen for devotion is also a mystery. It does, however, seem that the annual feast and procession in honor of San Luis Gonzaga began shortly after the arrival in Albuquerque of the Jesuit priests in early 1868. They were invited by then Bishop Jean Baptiste Lamy, first Bishop of New Mexico, and assigned to the church of San Felipe Neri, Albuquerque's oldest church. San Felipe Neri was also the mother church to several missions up and down the Rio Grande River Valley from the village of Alameda on the north to Atrisco on the south. One can only assume that it was these new priests to Albuquerque who brought San Luis Gonzaga and began his devotion in New Mexico. In *Works and Days: A History of San Felipe Neri Church 1867-1895*, by Father Thomas J. Steele, S.J., the author quotes the obituary of the death of fourteen-year-old Crecencio Armijo y Romero in August,

1883, which mentioned that Crecencio was a member of the San Luis Gonzaga Sodality.*

La Plaza de Los Griegos, named for the family who settled the area, is situated about three miles north of Albuquerque and was founded in 1708 as a land grant given to Juan Griego for his service to the Spanish Crown. The name Griego in Spanish means "Greek" or "of Greek origin." The families who settled and still live in the area are direct descendants of Juan Griego, the Spanish Conquistadors and original settlers of Albuquerque, which was founded in 1706. Some of the earliest surnames in the village were those of Griego, Candelaria, García, Martínez, and Gutiérrez.

The Catholic faith was first brought to New Mexico in 1539 by Fray Marcos de Niza, the explorer priest sent by the Viceroy in Mexico City to investigate stories of what lay to the north. The following year, Coronado arrived, accompanied by several priests, for a grand reconnaissance of the territory. Two of those priests stayed behind when Coronado left in 1542 and were quickly martyred by the people they sought to serve. In 1598, more Spaniards and more missionaries arrived with Juan de Oñate in the first colonizing expedition, and, except for the twelve years following the Pueblo Revolt of 1680, New Mexico has had a Catholic missionary presence from that time until now.

The person who first began homage to San Luis in Los Griegos is believed to have been Juana Griego, daughter of Juan Griego and Ana Maria Griego. On January 7, 1867, she married Santiago Gutiérrez, son of Juan Gutiérrez and Manuela López, at the church of San Felipe Neri in Albuquerque. It was in their home that the homage to San Luis began. The location of the house where his feast was first celebrated was near the parish church of Our Lady of Guadalupe and not far from the home where the image is now kept in the westernmost part of the village. Juana Griego de Gutiérrez died on July 8, 1920, in Los Griegos at the age of 68. The devotion was continued by Juana's daughter, Carlota Gutiérrez. Carlota Gutiérrez, daughter of Santiago Gutiérrez and Juana Griego, was baptized at San Felipe Neri on May 13, 1872 , at the age of three days. On November 27, 1886 , at the age of fourteen, she married Reyes Martínez, son of José Desiderio Martínez and María Eulogia de Jesús Candelaria. Reyes Martínez died on May 9, 1907, at the age of forty-four, only seven days after the birth of his daughter, Bárbara. On November 28, 1907, Carlota Gutiérrez de Martínez married Pablo Candelaria, also known as Pablo Apodaca. Pablo was born to Salamin Candelaria and Trinidad Griego, but was adopted by Isidro Apodaca and Symphoriana Griego, thus the name change from Candelaria to Apodaca. Carlota Gutiérrez de Apodaca died on May 13, 1946, at the age of seventy-four. By then the devotion had been passed on to her daughter, Bárbara Martínez, who was baptized at San Felipe Neri on May 5, 1907, at the age of two days. On November 15, 1922, at the age of fifteen, she became the wife of Teodoro Padilla. Bárbara Martínez de Padilla died on March 7, 1966, at the age of fifty-nine. Frances Padilla, daughter of Bárbara and Teodoro, now owns the home; and she, her sisters and brothers, Juanita Jaramillo, Dolores Inge, Pauline Duran, Teodoro Padilla, Jr., and Simón Padilla, have carried on the traditional homage to San Luis to this day.

The home, situated on one of the main village streets, has what one would call two living rooms. Both rooms are the same size, both face the street, and they are covered by a *portal* (front porch) with a door entering each room. The room to the left as one faces the house is the actual living room of the home. The room on the right-hand side is devoted to San Luis. A three-tiered altar of pine made by Juan Candelaria, brother of Pablo Candelaria Apodaca, sits in the center of the west wall. A twelve-inch plaster-of-Paris statue of San Luis sits at the top of the altar surrounded by candlesticks, silk flowers, and vases, all brought to him by pilgrims. Chairs line three walls of the room, and on either side of the main altar in the corners are fern tables covered with tablecloths on which sit statues of various saints. Hanging on the walls are pictures of saints, some old, some new. It seems that for generations people have brought the saint gifts.

Each year on his feast day the annual procession, rosaries, and dances in honor of San Luis are held. In the early morning hours the door to his room is opened for the public to enter. A family member is always present should anyone wish to pray and dance to San Luis, as the dancing is always led by a family member. The statue is placed on a ribbon-and-flower-decorated *andita* (a covered litter for carrying a statue), and a candlelight procession with the rosary prayed and sung in Spanish is held at sunset. The procession, which once was led through the village, now centers around the Padilla residence. Upon returning to the home, the statue is placed back in its *nicho* (niche); and the final prayers are said, intentions asked for, and a hymn of eight stanzas is sung to San Luis in Spanish. The pilgrims are then led back outside, where they all remove their shoes, and at the doorstep to his room the dance and hymn known as "La Indita" begins and continues in front of his altar. "La Indita," which is thirteen stanzas long, is again sung in Spanish, and the dance is performed after each stanza. At the end of all the ceremonies, Spanish hymns are continued throughout the evening until all the guests have left.

The feast day of San Luis was celebrated a little more elaborately in the early part of this century and was a true community event. Several days before the actual feast day, preparation of food began, as a very large number of people were expected and all were fed. During the day, the novena to San Luis was prayed. Those attending for only a short visit prayed three "Our Fathers" and danced a short version of "La Indita." Indians from the nearby Pueblo of Sandia came with great devotion, in wagons, and camped on the property for the vespers and feast day. The *ancianos* (old timers) of the neighborhood remember the Indians dancing "La Indita" in their native costumes in honor of San Luis, much to the delight of the local villagers.

In Los Griegos, San Luis Gonzaga is also known as the patron saint of single men — perhaps the reason for such great devotion to him by so many during the two World Wars, as it is said that mothers of soldiers came from all parts of the state, not only on his feast day but also during the year, to pray for the safe return of their sons.

During and after World War II, soldiers arriving back home from the war would call the home of Bárbara Padilla from the bus depot and, before they went to their own homes, ask if she would be so kind as to open the door to San Luis's room in order for them to give thanks for their safe return. One soldier, Eugene Seiler from the neighboring community of Martínez Town, brought sea shells from the Pacific Islands, where he was serving in the military, and made the *nicho* for the statue, in which it has been placed since the end of World War II.

In the middle part of this century Mrs. Cora Humphrey, one of the ladies from the village, began *Los Hijos de San Luis* (the Sons of San Luis) as a sodality for the young men of the community, but it unfortunately has not survived.

For over a hundred years, the descendants of Juana Griego and the people of Los Griegos have kept the celebration of the feast day of San Luis alive. The annual devotion is made up of young and old, and there is every indication that this homage will continue for many years to come.

From "*La Indita á San Luis Gonzaga*":

> *Desde México he venido*
> (From Mexico I have come)
> *A buscar este lugar*
> (Searching for this place)
> *Demen razón de San Luis*
> (Inform me regarding San Luis)
> *Que le prometí bailar.*
> (For I promised him I would dance.)

NOTE

* *Revista Católica* 9 #32 (11 August, 1883), 380-381.

XIII

The Splendid Flame
(For Aloysius Gonzaga,
Four Hundred Years Dead)

Clifford Stevens

The altar is baroque; the luminous lad
Hovers in silence above the candles' glow,
Determined, poised like the angelic host
About him, eyes lifted to that realm
Where he had sent his heart with fierce intent
Long, long before his childhood sun had set.

His was a soul of gold, furnaced and fired
Amid the frenzied palaces and ornamented halls
Where pride holds court and which with bold finality
He flung aside, clung to his God in agony,
And let the kingdoms of this world go up in flames.

This boy, the pride of the Gonzaga race,
The princeling of his clan, wrapped round
With silk and ermine and the trappings
Of his blood and state, the tiger-lily,
Knew well the poisoned field from which he sprung,
Held out his trembling hands to Him Whose own
Burned red upon the cross, and held them fast
Through rain and raging storm, through nights
Bloodied with his soul's deep anguished cry.

From out the jungle of his early years, there came
The certain call, faint, indistinct at first,
Then with the thunder of resolve, in Spain,

Entangled in the etiquette and protocol that bound
The princes of Escorial, in fair Madrid, upon the steps
That housed Ignatius' sons, he sat himself,
And he would sit, he said, until the doors
Were opened wide for him and he was bound with jesses
To his Lord, from which no earthly power could tear him.

And then, the darker struggle for his soul,
As promises were made, then broken, made
And broken again, reviled and banished
From his father's house, his freedom won,
Then lost, then won and lost again. And finally,
The chains were loosed, miraculously, he thought,
The bird took flight, and on the Quirinal, alone,
His heart's desire achieved at last, he knelt
In that blessed place: "This is my rest," he said.
"Here will I dwell, for I have chosen it."

And now, the fiercer fire that burned inside
Consumed him, as he romped before his Lord,
And hungered for the face of God. The magnitude
Of all that he had sought engulfed him, crushed him
With its wonder as it drew him into quiet corners
Where he knelt in awe, enwrapped in silence,
Or to that flaming furnace of desire towards which
With hurried steps his hunger drew him.

* * *

And then, from out the blackened countrysides
The caravans of starving peasants came, eyes filled with
        death,
Their bodies festering with disease. They filled
The tortuous streets and died by hundreds in the stifling
Wards where beds were few, the reek and smell
        unbearable

157

As death lurked everywhere and brave men brought some
    comfort
To the few who sat bewildered in their beds.

He saw the bleeding Christ in every face, begged alms
From princes in the streets, his childhood friends,
Or from the cardinals who passed in liveried elegance.
He lifted dying men in his frail arms, tended and nursed
Them till their breath was gone, bound up
Their festering wounds, held them as brothers,
Dear to him as Christ.

Then when it seemed he was invulnerable to pain,
To weariness, fatigue, to all that would deter him
From his task, and even from the danger of disease,
He was struck down, and joyfully himself lay down
Upon a bed of pain, and saw with certainty
The day of his deliverance before him.

He lay there through the weeks of Lent,
Eyes bright, his eyes upon the Christ he sought
With such deep passion, his mind sent heavenward,
His body wasting but his spirit keen, his mind alert
To friends and fellows. The splendid flame burned bright,
This lad, who pierced the heavens with his cries
From Mantua to Spain, who longed for God
And clung to Him with such devotion, making old men
Marvel and setting Italy ablaze with rumor,
Who grasped the cross and wrapped himself around
With every bond that love could fashion, lay in quiet
Expectation as the hymns of Corpus Christi faded
And the night enfolded him.

The splendid flame burned out and left a glow
That lingers even now, as we, across the centuries,
Reach out and grasp his hand.

About the Contributors

Father Daniel Berrigan, S.J., poet, playwright, controversialist, and antiwar activist (The Catonsville Nine, etc.), is with the West Side Jesuit Community in New York City and was technical advisor for the Academy Award-nominated film *The Mission*, about Jesuit missionary reductions in Latin America.

Martin Blair is director of public relations for Station WCBS-TV, New York, and a free-lance writer and editor in New York City.

Father Walter J. Burghardt, S.J., senior fellow of Woodstock Theological Center, former professor of patristics and theologian in residence at Georgetown University, has published a number of books including *Saints and Sanctity*.

Charles Carrillo, a well-known artist and *santero* in Santa Fe, New Mexico, painted the *retablo* of St. Aloysius Gonzaga in this book.

Richard C. Hermes, S.J., a Jesuit scholastic in St. Louis when he wrote about the concepts of the biographer Cepari, is completing study for the priesthood in New Orleans.

Cornelia Jessey, who traces Sts. Ignatius and Aloysius from *Don Quixote* to the present, lives in Oceanside, California, and is author of *The Prayer of Cosa: Praying in the Way of Francis of Assisi.*

Father Peter-Hans Kolvenbach, S.J., superior general of the Society of Jesus, occasioned this work by mentioning the fourth centenary of the death of St. Aloysius Gonzaga in the closing months of the Ignatian Year, 1990-1991.

Father William Hart McNichols, S.J., co-editor who completed this book, contributing the opening poem, an essay, drawings, and dust-jacket painting, is a poet-artist now working on Byzantine icons in Albuquerque, New Mexico.

Dan Paulos, whose frontispiece is an original paper-cutting of St. Aloysius for this book, is an artist and writer in Albuquerque, New Mexico.

Father M. Basil Pennington, O.C.S.O., author of works in various fields, has been visiting Cistercian communities in Hong Kong and Africa.

Ethel Pochocki, author of the Grandma Bagley and Brooksville Bunch stories and other children's books, lives in Brooks, Maine.

Andrés J. Segura, who describes a unique local devotion to St. Aloysius, chronicles the history of the Spanish community in Albuquerque, New Mexico.

Father Clifford Stevens, a former Air Force chaplain, founder of the Tintern monastic complex in Nebraska, and author of many works of fiction and nonfiction, was the initiating editor of this book, contributing the introductory essay and closing poem.

Father Joseph N. Tylenda, S.J., author and translator of many works on hagiography and spirituality, is with the Historical Institute of the Society of Jesus in Rome.

Wendy M. Wright, a member of the theology faculty of Creighton University in Omaha, Nebraska, is author of *Bond of Perfection*, a study of St. Francis de Sales and St. Jane Frances de Chantal.